MW00699302

GENOCIDE IN NIGERIA
The Ogoni Tragedy

By the same Author:

Novels
Sozaboy: A Novel in Rotten English
Basi and Company: A Modern African Folktale
Prisoners of Jebs
Pita Dumbrok's Prison

Short Stories
A Forest of Flowers
Adaku and Other Stories

Poetry
Songs in a Time of War

Drama
Basi and Company: Four Television Plays
Four Farcical Plays

General
On A Darkling Plain: An Account of the Nigerian Civil War
Nigeria: The Brink of Disaster
Similia: Essays on Anomic Nigeria

Children's Books
Tambari
Tambari in Dukana
Mr B
Mr B Again
Mr B is Dead
Mr B Goes to Lagos
The Transistor Radio
Segi Finds the Radio
A Shipload of Rice

Folklore
The Singing Anthill: Ogoni Folk Tales

GENOCIDE IN NIGERIA
The Ogoni Tragedy

Ken Saro-Wiwa

Saros International Publishers
London. Lagos. Port Harcourt

First published in 1992 by
Saros International Ltd.
24 Aggrey Road
Port Harcourt
Rivers State
Nigeria
Email: sarosintl@yahoo.com

Reissue 2005

Distributed outside Africa by
African Books Collective, Oxford
www.africanbookscollective.com

Michigan State University Press
www.msupress.msu.edu

British Library Cataloguing in Publication Data
This data is available from the British Library.

ISBN 1 870716 22 1

Printed by Lightning Source

CONTENTS

Cover: Scenes from Bomu Blow-out 1970

To the Memory of T. N. Paul Birabi, Ogoni patriot.

AUTHOR'S NOTE

Writing this book has been one of the most painful experiences of my life. Ordinarily, writing a book is torture, a chore. But when, on every page, following upon every word, every letter, a tragedy leaps up before the eyes of a writer, he or she cannot derive that pleasure, that fulfillment in which the creative process often terminates.

What has probably worsened the matter is that I have lived through most of the period covered by this sordid story. I knew, as a child, that period from 1947 when the Ogoni saw, for a few brief years, the possibility of extricating themselves from the cruel fate which seems to have been ordained for them. I watched as they went into decline. I was privileged to play a role in the civil war which decimated them further and to assist in their rehabilitation at the end of that war.

Since then I have watched helplessly as they have been gradually ground to dust by the combined effort of the multi-national oil company, Shell Petroleum Development Company, the murderous ethnic majority in Nigeria and the country's military dictatorships. Not the pleas, not the writing over the years have convinced the Nigerian elite that something special ought to be done to relieve the distress of the Ogoni.

I have known and argued earnestly since I was a lad of seventeen that the only way the Ogoni can survive is for them to exercise their political and economic rights. But because the Nigerian elite appear, on this particular matter, to have hearts of stone and the brains of millipedes; because Shell is a multi-national company with the ability to crush whomever it wishes; because the petroleum resources of the Ogoni serve everyone's greed, all the doors seemed closed.

Three recent events have encouraged me to now place the issue before the world: the end of the Cold War, the increasing attention being paid to the global environment, and the insistence of the European Community that minority rights be respected, albeit in the successor states to the Soviet Union and in Yugoslavia. What remains to be seen is whether Europe and America will apply in Nigeria the same standards which they have applied in Eastern Europe.

For what has happened and is happening to the Ogoni is strictly not

7

the fault of the Nigerian elite and Shell Company alone; the international community has played a very significant role in it. If the Americans did not purchase Nigerian oil, the Nigerian nation would not be, nor would the oppressive ethnic majority in the country have the wherewithal to pursue its genocidal intentions. Indeed, there is a sense in which the "Nigerian" oil which the Americans, Europeans and Japanese buy is stolen property: it has been seized from its owners by force of arms and has not been paid for. Therefore, these buyers are receiving stolen property. Also, it is Western investment and technology which keep the Nigerian oil industry and therefore the Nigerian nation alive, oil being 94 per cent of Nigeria's Gross Domestic Product.

Also, European and American shareholders in multi-national oil companies and manufacturers of oil mining equipment have benefitted from the purloining of Ogoni resources, the devastation of the Ogoni environment and the genocide of the Ogoni people.

Thus, shareholders in the multi-national oil companies - both Shell and Chevron - which prospect for oil in Ogoni, the American, Japanese and European Governments, and the multi-national oil companies have a moral if not legal responsibility for ending the genocide of the Ogoni people and the complete devastation of their environment, if, indeed, that is still possible.

The requirement is enormous and urgent. The Ogoni people themselves including their children are determined to save whatever is left of their rich heritage. The international community can support this determination by championing the drive of the Ogoni for autonomy within Nigeria. The restoration of their rights, political, economic and environmental does not, cannot, hurt anyone. It will only place the responsibility for ending this dreadful situation where it should lie: on the Ogoni people themselves. The area being rich in resources and the people resourceful, the Ogoni will be able to sort out their problem in time.

Secondly, the international community must prevail on Shell and Chevron which prospect for oil in Ogoni, and the Nigerian Government which abets them, to stop flaring gas in the area immediately.

Thirdly, the international community can help by sending experts - medical, environmental and agricultural - to assist the Ogoni people restore a semblance of normality to Ogoni territory.

In the early years of this century, a French writer, André Gide, toured the Congo and observed the gross abuse of human rights being perpetrated in that country by King Leopold II of Belgium and his agents. He wrote about it and Europeans were sufficiently shocked to end the abuses.

I write now in the hope that the international community will, in similar fashion, do something to mitigate the Ogoni tragedy. It is bad enough that it is happening a few years into the twenty-first century. It will be a disgrace to humanity should it persist one day longer.

I expect the ethnic majority in Nigeria to turn the heat of their well-known vindictiveness on me for writing this book. I defy them to do so.

Some may wonder at my use of the word 'genocide' to describe what has happened to the Ogoni people. The United Nations defines genocide as "the commission of acts with intent to destroy a national, ethnic, racial or religious group". If anyone, after reading this book, has any further doubt of, or has a better description for, the crime against the Ogoni people, I will be happy to know it.

I wish to thank Barika Idamkue and Dr Sonpie Kpone-Tonwe for kindly reading the manuscript and making valuable suggestions for improving the work; and my assistant, Hyacinth Wayi, for speedy word-processing.

All errors in the book are mine and I accept full responsibility for them.

Ken Saro-Wiwa
Port Harcourt, 1992.

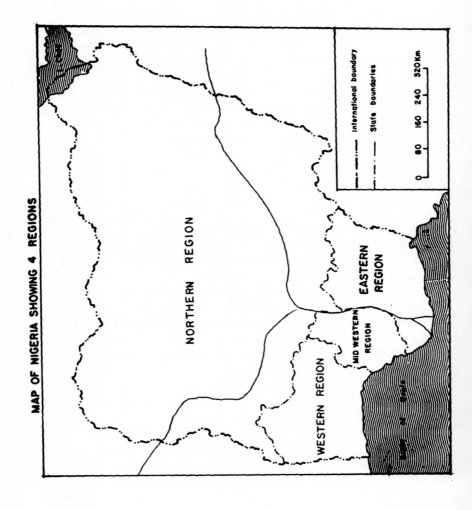

MAP OF NIGERIA SHOWING 4 REGIONS

CHAPTER 1

BACKGROUND

The Ogoni are a distinct ethnic group within the Federal Republic of Nigeria. Their territory forms the easternmost extension of the mainland fringe bordering the eastern Niger delta, lying in an area between approximately latitude 4.05' and 4.20' north and longitudes 7.10' and 7.30' east.

Covering a total of approximately 404 square miles, it forms part of the coastal plains terrace which here appears as a gently sloping plateau. The central part of this plateau is about 100 feet above sea level. It has an estimated population of 500,000.

There is yet much anthropological, ethnographic, sociological and linguistic work to be done to determine the true origins of the Ogoni people. One theory is that they migrated into the area from across the Imo River (Two Ogoni villages, Warife and Utetuk still exist on the eastern side of the Imo). A second theory is that the Ogoni came in boats from Ghana and settled in the southern part of the area. Believers of this theory point to the name by which most of the Ogoni call themselves (Khana) as a pointer to the Ghana origins of the Ogoni people. Colonial administrators have pointed to the paucity of legends on the origin of the Ogoni and linguistic experts classify the Ogoni languages of Khana, Gokana and Eleme as a distinct group within the Benue-Congo branch of African languages or, more particularly, as a branch in the New Benue-Congo family.

Generally, the Ogoni are said to have settled in the area well before the fifteenth century and established themselves in the six kingdoms of Babbe, Eleme, Gokana, Nyo-Khana, Ken-Khana and Tai. The history which lies behind this is very interesting, but is of little value here.

What is of interest is that the Ogoni had inherited a precious part of God's earth and did everything to preserve it. The rich plateau soil provided agricultural plenty and the rivers which wash the borders of the entire area brimmed with fishes and sea food. The Ogoni seized the opportunity to become competent farmers and fishermen and to transform their territory into the food basket of the eastern Niger delta.

But what the Ogoni realized, from earliest times, was the necessity to preserve the territory for themselves, a task at which they were very ferocious, earning for themselves in the process, a reputation for "cannibalism". Throughout their recorded history, there is no instance of any of their neighbours being able to impose upon them in any manner whatsoever. They were never defeated in war and were not colonized by anyone except the British.

To the Ogoni, the land on which they lived and the rivers which surrounded them were very important. They not only provided sustenance in abundance, they were also a spiritual inheritance. The land is a god and is worshipped as such. The fruit of the land, particularly yams, are honoured in festivals and, indeed, the Annual Festival of the Ogoni is held at the yam harvest. The planting season is not a mere period of agricultural activity: it is a spiritual, religious and social occasion. "Tradition" in Ogoni means in the local tongue (*doonu kuneke*) the honouring of the land (earth, soil, water). This respect for the land means that forests are not merely a collection of trees and the abode of animals but also, and more intrinsically, a sacred possession. Trees in the forest cannot therefore be cut indiscriminately without regard for their sacrosanctity and their influence on the well-being of the entire community, of the land.

Moreover, the Ogoni believe that the soul of a man or woman has the power to leave its human form and enter into that of a beast, taking on the shape of an animal. G. N. Loolo, the Ogoni historian asserts in his study "A History of the Ogoni" (Port Harcourt, 1986) that, *nearly all "strong" animals in the bush, such as tiger, elephants, antelope, tortoise, and such aquatic animals as crocodiles, turtles and catfish are credited with being "were" beasts. It is a common belief that should any harm come to a "were" beast, it would also affect its human counterpart.*

To the Ogoni, rivers and streams do not only provide water for life - for bathing and drinking etc; they do not only provide fish for food, they are also sacred and are bound up intricately with the life of the community, of the entire Ogoni nation. As indicated above, they also contain animals into which the human soul can be transmuted. In some cases, they are deified, and erring human action can desecrate them and therefore bring disaster upon the people who are regarded as their custodians.

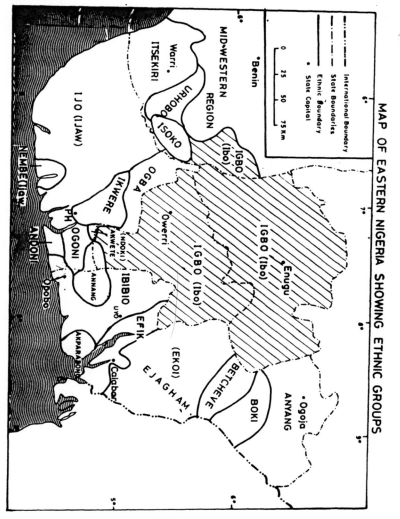

In modern times, this translates to a deep awareness of the importance of the environment and the necessity to protect and preserve it. The Ogoni ancients knew that the land which was their inheritance was rich farmland; that the fresh and salt water rivers which surrounded them were blessed with plenteousness. They did everything to preserve this rich inheritance.

Before the advent of the Atlantic Slave Trade, the Ogoni had established an organized social system which worked under a monarchy and under which men and women of courage and ability enjoyed a special status.

During the Slave Trade, the Ogoni lay on the slave route from the hinterland to the coastal slave markets. However, no Ogoni man or woman was taken as a slave. No record of the Ogoni languages exists in the *Polyglotta Africana,* the record of languages spoken by Africans taken into slavery in the New World. Indeed, there is evidence in the oral traditions of the Ogoni to suggest that the Ogoni considered slavery a disgrace to manhood. "I'd rather drown in the sea than be killed by an Ibani" is a well-known Ogoni proverb, indicating that the Ogoni would have nothing to do with the slave markets of Bonny. The slaves the Ogoni knew about were Igbos or "gbon" as the Ogoni called them. If an Ogoni man is given an unsavoury task, he will ask, *"m lu o gbon?"* (Am I your slave?)

The Ogoni also forbade intermarriage with all their neighbours except the Ibibio.

Thus, to the end of the Atlantic Slave Trade, the Ogoni were able to preserve their land and culture and maintain peace and order in their territory in virtual isolation.

However, contact with the inhuman trade introduced firearms to the area and in the later half of the nineteenth century, internecine wars became the order of the day. By 1900 these wars had virtually destroyed the fabric of Ogoni society and the Ogoni were forced to survive in independent villages. This was the condition in which the British colonialist found them in the early years of the twentieth century when the former began the free-lance colonization of eastern Nigeria.

CHAPTER 2

UNDER BRITISH RULE

Although Europeans had been in the Niger delta from as early as 1485, a combination of forces stopped them from coming into early contact with the Ogoni. The ferocity of the Ogoni and their reputation among their neighbours as "cannibals" may have contributed to this. The geographical location, far from the nearest anchorages of the European trading ships, was also a contributory factor. It was not until 1901 that colonial forces landed in Ogoni at Kono and Ogoni country was proclaimed a British protectorate.

But no effective presence was established in the area. The Ogoni resented this intrusion upon their lives and refused to accept British overlordship. In 1903 and again in 1905, the records speak of patrols being sent "to enforce administrative control" and of "a number of villages" being "destroyed".

Such wanton destruction of life and property was not acceptable to the Ogoni and they resisted it. In 1913, yet another attack was launched against the Ogoni. This finally broke the resistance and when, in 1914, the religious centre of the Ogoni at Ka-Gwara was razed to the ground by Major Webber and a large police escort under a Major G. H. Walker DS0, the Ogoni were finally subjugated.

It was in that same year that Nigeria came into being. In effect, at that time when the Ogoni were technically absorbed into a Nigeria created by the British, the Ogoni had not ceded their sovereignty.

For twenty years thereafter, the area was left to stagnate. The British did not establish an administration; the Ogoni nation was administered as a part of Opobo Division within the Calabar Province. The divisional headquarters was separated from Ogoni by the Imo River and Calabar was about 200 miles away. British rule of the area was "haphazard".

To the Ogoni, British administration meant the collection of taxes and the establishment of courts for the maintenance of law and order.

No more. The taxes collected were not used for the benefit or improvement of Ogoni. The Primitive Methodist Mission established a church at Kono and the Anglican Church began to operate in the area. One or two schools were established by these churches through local effort. Once in a while, an Assistant District Officer would pay a visit to the area to sit over court cases, parcel out Ogoni land to their Igbo neighbours or enforce the collection of taxes.

By 1929, the tax burden had become so unbearable that the women of Ogoni joined in the Women's Tax Riots of that year. Several Ogoni women were killed during the quelling of the riots at Egwanga, (now Ikot Abasi) the Opobo Divisional headquarters.

It had by now become obvious that the Ogoni had to be better administered. In 1914, an Assistant Divisional Officer, Mr D. Murphy had been specifically assigned to take charge of Ogoni country. In 1925, Mr Gibbons took over from him, completed an "Intelligence Report" and made recommendations for the better administration of law and order. In his 1932 report, he wrote:

> *British rule has penetrated so little below the surface of Ogoni organization during the last thirty years that in many respects the country is more or less as it was before the advent of government. Lawlessness is to be found everywhere ... The reasons for the foregoing are obvious, and Mr Falk in the provincial Annual Report for 1930 is of the opinion that the absence of contact with civilization has been a boon rather than the reverse.*

> *I now wish to emphatically reiterate the considered opinion of not only myself but of the other District Officers who have been in charge of the Opobo Division that no real success can attend to the administration of this large tribe until the local organization, placed on proper footing, is guided by a European officer of experience and stationed permanently in the area, to replace the haphazard method of occasional visits from Opobo which has hitherto been in force.*

Mr Gibbons took in hand the construction of a road to link Kono with the newly-established town of Port Harcourt. This road had the effect of opening up Ogoni for the first time to the outside world. The road was completed in 1935. In that same year, Mr M. D. W. Jeffreys succeeded Mr Gibbons. Unlike his predecessors, Mr Jeffreys lived at Bori, the headquarters of the Ogoni nation.

The Second World War in 1939 attracted several Ogoni men into the foreign legion of the British Army. The end of the war presaged the nationalist struggle for independence and freedom in Nigeria.

In Ogoni, there was already a demand for the creation of a separate administrative division. The demand was spearheaded by the Ogoni Central Union of which all village chiefs and literate youths were members. The argument was that the Ogoni were a distinct ethnic group with its own language and culture and that their population was large enough to merit a separate administrative division. This demand received additional impetus after the end of the war. By the Constitutional Amendment Orders-in-Council of 1946, the Ogoni Division was created and included in a Rivers Province whose creation the Ogoni people had demanded alongside the peoples of the delta and its northern fringes.

When in 1947 the Ogoni Native Authority was established, the Ogoni had, after almost 50 years of British colonialism, come into their own once again. Under the moral leadership of T. N. Paul Birabi, who had studied at Achimota College (in Ghana) and the University of Southampton (where he graduated in Mathematics in 1948), the Ogoni began to re-establish themselves. The Ogoni Central Union established a University scholarship scheme under which two students, Messrs S. F. Nwika and Kemte Giadom studied in the United States of America. The Union also engaged in other business activities in an effort to raise funds. Levies were also made towards the establishment of the first secondary school in the area.

By 1950, T. N. Paul Birabi had recognized the fact that the Ogoni needed not only good administration but fundamentally, ethnic autonomy. He therefore inaugurated the Ogoni State Representative Assembly (OSRA). It was his idea that the Ogoni should have self-determination alongside other ethnic groups within the burgeoning Nigerian Federation. And it was on this platform that the Ogoni people returned him unopposed to the newly-formed Eastern House of Assembly at Enugu, whence he proceeded to the House of Representatives in Lagos.

I was growing up in Bori, the headquarters of the Ogoni people at this time of incipient Ogoni autonomy and can bear witness to how the Ogoni took their fortune in their own hands.

Ogoni was always a blessed land. The plateau soil was extremely rich, the fresh water streams and the surrounding seas brimmed with fish, the forests had an abundance of animals and hard woods preserved by the environment-conscious Ogoni (my father was a forest-ranger) and the Ogoni were extremely hardworking. We were very well fed and the Ogoni people lacked for nothing.

Although the Ogoni had come into late contact with western civilization, the chiefs who sat in the Ogoni Native Authority took in hand the propulsion of the Ogoni nation into the twentieth century. The Ogoni people established primary schools themselves through the Christian missions; Ogoni languages were taught in schools, the New Testament was translated into Khana (one of the Ogoni languages); the General Hospital at Bori was built and a string of dispensaries was established in each of the five Ogoni kingdoms; the Ogoni people began to levy themselves to set up the first secondary school in the area - what has now become Birabi Memorial Grammar School.

I have since met (in England) Mr Fitzroy Somerset who was the last but one British District Officer in Ogoni. He left Ogoni in 1956 and confirms the ease with which the Ogoni people were administered and how quick on the uptake the people were. He informs me how well the Chiefs served their people and attests to the success which attended their efforts.

Alas, all this was not to last, thanks to the intrusion of Nigeria. Because while the Ogoni were struggling to pull themselves into the twentieth century, the Nigeria which the British had created and into which the Ogoni had been forced willy-nilly, was planning to drive them to extinction. The manner of it deserves some attention.

CHAPTER 3

THE NIGERIAN INTRUSION

When the British brought Nigeria into being in 1914, they had put together a great number of ethnic groups with widely differing languages, cultures and histories - including the history of their contact with the British. In the words of one of its early Governors, Sir Hugh Clifford, Nigeria is "a mere collection of self-contained and mutually-independent Native States, separated from one another ... by great distances, by differences of history and tradition and by ethnological, racial, tribal, political, social and religious barriers". And in 1955, Lord Malcolm Hailey, the British historian described Nigeria as "perhaps the most artificial of the many administrative units created in the course of European occupation of Africa."

The only thing which kept the disparate peoples together was force. British force. Without this force, there would not have been a Nigeria. Even with that force, the country remained a "notoriously precarious lumping together" of unwilling peoples.

There was truly no rational way you could justify, for instance, the Yoruba, numerous, with a long tradition of contact with western Europe and of western education dating back to 1832, being lumped with the few Ogoni who had had no real contact with the outside world until 1935.

Inevitable tension was the result of this misadventure and this tension was managed with much skill and argument backed by force.

Since British interest in Nigeria was mainly economic, the desires and well-being of each particular Nigerian group did not matter.

Until the 1930s, most educated Nigerians came from Yoruba families which had had long contact with Europeans. Along with Creole families which had settled in Lagos, they formed a formidable aristocracy with whom no other "Nigerians" could compete. When that competition arrived, the Ogoni people were not there. To all intents and purposes, therefore, the interest of the Ogoni was not considered in the burgeoning politics of the period.

A number of Constitutional proposals were put in place, and Nigeria gradually moved towards a federalism predicated on three Regions. The dominant feature of the Regional arrangement was the preponderance of one ethnic group or ruling class in each of the Regions: the Yorubas in the Western Region, the Igbos in the Eastern Region and the Hausa-Fulani in the Northern Region. These three groups, Hausa-Fulani, Igbo and Yoruba became the power-brokers in Nigeria, with the minority ethnic groups in each Region attached to them as mere appendages. Predictably, these three groups were to struggle for control of the nation and its resources while the 300-odd minority groups were left to pick the crumbs or struggle for independence from the control (or indigenous colonialism) of the majority groups in each Region.

While the British ruled Nigeria, the minorities felt relatively safe but as Nigeria moved towards independence, it became fairly obvious that they were imperilled and that they would have to do something to save themselves. Hence the major effort of the minority ethnic groups was canalized, not towards economic development, but towards a political settlement which, it was rightly seen, would presage economic development.

Two schools of thought emerged as to how best the ethnic groups could co-exist in the country. There were those who believed that the differences between the ethnic groups were fixed and that the only way to combat the artificial creation which was Nigeria was to devolve government on the ethnic groups. Others believed that politics should be seen in terms of Nigeria and not its ethnic components and that ethnic politics should be discouraged.

In the denouement, what was achieved was a mixed bag. The Regional arrangement preached unitarism within the Region while proposing federalism in the country. It contained within itself the seeds of its own destruction.

For instance, in 1948, the Yoruba met and proclaiming that they would "not be relegated to the background in the future", declared their objective to be "to create and foster the idea of a single nationalism throughout Yorubaland" and to "co-operate with existing ethnical and regional associations and such as may exist hereafter, in matters of common interest to all Nigerians so as thereby to attain unity in federalism."

At the same time, the Igbos under Azikiwe declared: "It would appear that the God of Africa has created the Igbo nation to lead the children of Africa from the bondage of the ages ..."

In 1953, the Hausa-Fulani in the Northern Region demanded the dissolution of the Federation and the devolution of government on the Regions which were to be linked only by a central agency of a non-political character appointed jointly by the Regional governments.

Such latent differences and antagonisms did not augur well for the unitary systems that were foisted on the Regions. Nor did they indicate that federalism at the centre would work smoothly.

By 1954, however, all the cracks had been papered over and preparations began for a new Constitution which would lead Nigeria to independence. The Constitution which emerged re-inforced regionalism and although the minority ethnic groups in each of the Regions made it clear that they wanted self-determination and autonomy, it was felt that that could be sorted out after independence which should not be delayed on any account.

In March 1945, the Sir Richards Constitution had contained certain Ordinances which, in line with British economic interests, vested mineral rights and publicly purchased lands in the Crown. This was a major bone of contention even at that time. For corporate ownership of land by lineages remains fundamental to the traditional structure of most Nigerian societies. Therefore, customary land law opposed the disruption which British rule and its new economic order occasioned. Customary law also prevented economic exploitation of the land by individual Nigerians.

In the pre-independence Constitution this niggling matter received some mitigation. To enforce the rights of communities to their land, it was agreed that mining taxes should be federally collected and distributed to the Regions on the basis of derivation.

More exactly, the Independence Constitution of 1960 spelt out clearly the principles of sharing revenue derived from each part of the Federation:

There shall be paid by the Federation to each Region a sum equal to fifty per cent of

(a)   *the proceeds of any royalty received by the Federation in respect of any minerals extracted in that Region; and*

(b)   *any mining rents derived by the Federation within that Region.*

The formation of the Ogoni State Representative Assembly in 1950 was in accord with the actions of most of Nigeria's ethnic groups at the time.

The Yoruba had their *Egbe Omo Oduduwa*, the Igbo their Ibo State Union, the Ibibio their Ibibio State Union which was established as far back as 1928, and the Hausa their *Jammiyyar Mutanen Arewa*. When Birabi took his seat in the House of Representatives in 1952, the Ogoni found themselves for the first time in the mainstream of Nigerian politics. He died soon after attending the Conference on the Nigerian Constitution held in London in July and August of the next year, 1953.

In 1957 the Eastern Region became self-governing. I have it on the authority of Fitzroy Somerset quoted earlier that when Sir James Robertson, the last British Governor of Nigeria visited Ogoni in 1956, the Chiefs made it clear to him that they did not want to be a part of the Eastern Region. The Governor was not impressed.

All the same, the Ogoni under the leadership of Messrs S. F. Nwika and Kemte Giadom continued to press for the creation of a Rivers State that would group the minority ethnic groups of the delta including Ogoni.

At that time the minority ethnic groups in the Eastern Region felt, and not without reason, that the only way they could escape the chauvinism of the Igbo ethnic majority to whose rule they had been consigned by Regionalism was to band up against the Igbo. The self-determination of these minorities was strongly urged on the colonial authorities which reacted by setting up the Sir Henry Willink Commission of Inquiry which was to investigate the fears of the minorities and seek ways of allaying them.

The Commission found itself "unable to recommend any new State in this (Eastern) Region." Its reasons were that the proposed Rivers State was not viable ("To sever themselves from the wealthier parts of the Region is surely not the way to get the schools and floating dispensaries they want") and that the creation of such a state "would be sharply resented by the Ibos of the central plateau."

The British Secretary of State for the Colonies in London did recognize *that the present Regional boundaries and number of Regions could not be regarded as standing for all time and accordingly commended to the Conference proposals which he tabled, for a procedure to be included in the Constitution for Independence for effecting boundary changes and creating new Regions.*

But the proposals which emerged were most disappointing. No states could be created out of any Region, *except with the approval of that Region!*

As the Willink Commission was to find, the creation of Rivers State would be "sharply resented" by the Igbos.

In effect, the Ogoni and the other minorities of the Eastern delta had been consigned to colonial status at the hands of the Igbo ethnic majority. As a sop, these ethnic minorities were offered a Niger Delta Development Board as recommended by the Willink Commission.

The Board was well-conceived but it was still-born, since all it could do was carry out research and make recommendations to the Regional and Federal Governments. In its six or seven years of life, it achieved nothing whatsoever.

Thus, when Nigeria became independent in 1960, the scene had been set for (1) competitive Federalism at the centre between the three major ethnic groups - Hausa, Igbo and Yoruba - and (2) a battle for self-determination by the minorities in the Regions. The new nation was set for war with itself!

The dilemma of the Ogoni was beyond description. They had only begun to establish themselves in 1947. In 1951, Nigerian nationalists, particularly Dr Nnamdi Azikiwe and Mbonu Ojike of the National Council of Nigeria and the Cameroons (NCNC) party had barnstormed the area preaching freedom. Sang Mbonu Ojike:

> *Everywhere there must be freedom.*
> *Freedom for you*
> *Freedom for me*
> *Everywhere, there must be freedom.*
> *Freedom! Freedom!*
> *Everywhere there must be freedom.*

The Ogoni reacted to this call by voting for the NCNC party.

In 1957, they were before the Willink Commission of Inquiry arguing for freedom in a Rivers State which was to be excised from Eastern Nigeria. This earned them much derision and physical molestation at the hands of the Igbo ethnic majority who resented the exercise of a fundamental right. In a reaction to this, when the Eastern House of Assembly was dissolved later that year and a new election presaging Regional self-government took place, the Ogoni voted for the opposition Action Group party. The successful party, the NCNC, led by the Igbos, took reprisals against the Ogoni, denying them scholarships and social amenities.

By this time, a Commission of Enquiry had reviewed Native Authority Administration in the Region and the highly successful Ogoni Native Authority was split into three local government units. The Ogoni sun had begun to set even before it had risen. The road to decline was clearly marked.

The mere decline might have been reversed in time if extinction was not to follow it. Extinction arrived in the form of the multi-national oil company, Shell-B.P. It arrived in Ogoni not even bothering to wave the oil mining lease (OML) which it had obtained from the colonial administration under the ordinance which appropriated all minerals found in the colony to the Crown.

The Ogoni were hardly aware of the import of the oil company to their lives. The legislation covering the mining of oil was rudimentary. Little or no compensation was to be paid to the owners of the land on which oil was found and the oil company could pretty much do whatever it pleased in the search for oil.

In 1958, oil was struck in commercial quantity in Dere (misnamed Bomu oilfield) in the Gokana kingdom of Ogoni. The result of this find will form the subject of chapter 5 of this book.

CHAPTER 4

CIVIL WAR

Nigerian independence in 1960 was to exacerbate all the latent differences and tensions in the multi-ethnic nation. As indicated in the previous chapter, the seeds of destruction had been sown in the political structuring of the nation which established three Regions in a federation while leaving the Regions as unitary states. The country had virtually been handed over to the three major ethnic groups - Hausa-Fulani, Igbo and Yoruba - to do pretty much whatever they liked with it. The interest of the 300-odd other ethnic groups, including the Ogoni was not taken into account. The informing spirit of this arrangement was clearly stated by Margery Perham in a foreword to Obafemi Awolowo's *Path to Nigerian Freedom* (London, Faber & Faber, 1947):

> *Each of the three main groups should now be able to develop further its special capacities. The Hausa have their large and historic city-states and their Islamic traditions of law and discipline. The Yoruba have their happy and fertile marriage of aristocratic and democratic principles and of urban and rural societies. The Ibos, lacking in social cohesion, supply their equalitarian outlook and intense individual vitality. If the new Nigerian Constitution can express and develop the special virtues of the main groups, each of these might well make, out of its component societies, a unit sufficient in size, numbers and its unified culture, to rank some day as a nation. If, however, the main groups can come together at the centre to pool, and share their traditions and resources, whether through a Federal or a Unitary system, then there may some day be a Nigeria which will be a leading power on the African continent and might make Africa's main contribution in the international sphere.*

The Hausa, Yoruba and Ibo politicians took Margery Perham seriously. They got together at the centre, not to "pool and share their traditions and resources" but to use their presence to secure for their Regions (for which read "themselves") the resources jointly contributed by all Nigerian groups in a bid, it seems, to each "rank some day as a nation."

The way to this was, first, the mobilization of each of these majority ethnic groups and the exploitation of the resources and weakness of the minorities whom history had placed at their disposal. A regional community necessarily developed in all Regions; however, the minorities were severely disadvantaged. These minorities were not about to accept this.

Obafemi Awolowo in *Path to Nigerian Freedom*, had warned: *Certainly these minority groups are at a considerable disadvantage when they are forced to be in the midst of other peoples who differ from them in language, culture and historical background. And he had added, Under a true Federal Constitution, each group, however small, is entitled to the same treatment as any other group, however large. Opportunity must be afforded to each to evolve its own peculiar political institution.*

In the competition for Federal power, the minorities in each Region began to group against the major ethnic groups, to challenge their dominance and assert their own rights. Thus did the State Movements arise.

The Ogoni were in favour of the creation of Rivers State and continued to argue for it.

Meanwhile, the competition for Federal power between the major ethnic groups intensified. The upshot was the military coup d'état of 15th January, 1966 in which the Federal Prime Minister, Sir Abubakar Tafawa Balewa was killed along with two other Regional Premiers of the Yoruba and Hausa-Fulani ethnic majorities. As the leaders of that coup were Igbo and the succeeding ruler of the country, Major-General J. T. U. Aguiyi-Ironsi, was also Igbo, the Hausa-Fulani read ethnocentrism into it and took revenge, massacring Igbos and killing General Ironsi. Chaos resulted from this and, for a time, it looked as if the federation was about to end. The ethnic majorities were willing to see the break-up of the federation and put up arguments toward this.

The minorities on the other hand argued for the continued existence of the country and recommended the political re-structuring of the country through the creation of states. They won and succeeded in giving the nation another tenuous lifeline. But the Igbos under Colonel Odumegwu Ojukwu were not about to accept this. They went into rebellion and seceded from the federation, declaring a new republic of biafra.

The ill-fated republic was to group the Igbos and the ethnic minorities in what was Eastern Nigeria. As may be expected, these minorities, including the Ogoni, resented the attempt to corral them willy-nilly into a new and untested nation where they would most likely be treated as slaves. The words of Colonel Ojukwu, the rebel leader whose masturbatory egoism, intransigence and political illiteracy was to wreak so much horror on the peoples of Eastern Nigeria are revealing:

> *I arranged for and met in long sessions, and on separate occasions, representations from the Old Calabar Province, the old Rivers Province, and the representatives of the Old Ogoja Province. At these meetings the people spoke out their minds boldly, frankly and fearlessly. They complained that they lacked a sense of belonging, owing to the attitude of the majority group (the Igbos).*
>
> *They pointed to alleged injustices which they had suffered in the distribution of amenities, the siting of industries, and appointments to public offices, banks and corporations. They therefore felt that a separate state for them would cure all those ills ... I was finally left with the impression, and this applied practically to all the groups with whom I had discussed, that all they wanted was to feel that they belong, on a perfect footing of equality, to the Eastern Nigerian community, where all vestiges and grounds of domination of one group by another are removed, where social amenities and other government benefits are fairly and justly distributed. I expressed an honest sympathy with, and understanding of, their feelings and assured them that it was precisely those types of things that the military government was here to put right.*

Ojukwu was lying, as usual, in asserting that he meant to put things right. He went on to propose a "Provincial Administration System" under which "executive and legislative powers would be devolved on the provinces".

N. U. Akpan, Ojukwu's principal administrative adviser, himself a minority Ibibio, in his book, *The Struggle for Secession, 1966-70* (Frank Cass, 1971) has given an insight into the workings of biafra. According to him, the architects of the new system did not encourage open debates; they *set about their task in a clandestine way, paying nocturnal visits to different parts and people in the minority areas. It is said, and I cannot confirm or deny it, that some leaders in these areas were induced with money to support the proposals.*

In the end, although twenty provincial units and many more administrative divisions were created, it was all a farce. Ojukwu had a hidden agenda to the war. He wanted to control the oil of the Ogoni and other delta minorities. He calculated that if the resources of these people were in the hands of his new kingdom, the latter would be extremely well off.

The oil resources of the Ogoni and other delta minorities were also at the top of the consideration of the Federal Government. Consequently, the worst battles of the war were fought in this area, and the inhabitants thereof were to suffer the worst possible excesses of cruelty and dehumanization.

According to N. U. Akpan, *every Federal victory (in the minority areas) was ascribed to the work of saboteurs or lack of co-operation by the people in the areas concerned. And such people were molested and harassed.* Akpan reports that *Ojukwu gave tacit approval to acts of murder and arson committed against the minorities. His instructions were that once the Federal troops were known to be approaching an area, the first task of the Biafran troops and people was to move in there and bring out as many people as possible by force into the Biafran heartland. Those who would come out were friends, while others were to be regarded as enemies and treated as such.*

Akpan also reports as follows: *Port Harcourt was the last place whose fall led to the inhabitants being treated as saboteurs, and so cruelly treated. I went to Igrita shortly after the fall of Port Harcourt and was terribly shocked by the number of bodies being carted into mass graves-bodies of persons killed not by bullets but by cruel handling, and not by soldiers but by frenzied and ill-motivated civilians.*

Many of the murdered men and women whom Mr Akpan saw were Ogoni. For, Ogoni lay on the route of the Federal troops to Port Harcourt and suffered the full effects of Ojukwu's cruel order.

I was federal Administrator for the oil port of Bonny during the civil war and spent the months of June, July, August and September 1968 between Bonny, Ogoni and Port Harcourt. I have reported my experience in those months in my book, *On A Darkling Plain: An Account of the Nigerian Civil War* (Saros, 1989) and will quote therefrom:

I found that the greater majority of the Ogoni people had been evacuated from their homes and had gone or been shepherded into Iboland. They were mostly peasants - farmers and fishermen - who spoke no other language than their native Khana, Gokana or Eleme and had hardly ever stepped out of their home areas. Some had never as much as left their villages. And it was war time when the best and worst in the human psyche are brought out in full panoply.

Given the nature of the times, they could not expect to have a happy welcome among their hosts who, it must be stated, were under tremendous psychological stress, to put it mildly. Their plight is therefore better imagined than described.

In the three months during which I sojourned in my homeland with the help of the Federal troops who allowed me free movement and gave me transportation, I was to feel the full effect of what it means to be an extreme minority in the society that is Nigeria... The worry was for those who were in the Ibo heartland, in the rump of biafra.

For an insight as to what happened to them, I have to thank Peter Akere who is now a lawyer in Port Harcourt. I had taught him English Literature at Stella Maris College, Port Harcourt, in the second half of 1965, after my graduation from the University of Ibadan. He was one of the Ogoni who found themselves in the Ibo heartland after the liberation of Ogoni and Rivers State.

At war's end, I got him to write me an account of the sojourn of the Ogoni in Iboland between April 1968 and January 1970. His account is lucid and clear. I cross-checked his narration against a similar one which I commissioned from my relative, Sylvester Nwigbo (now a member of the Management staff of Pan-African Bank). The two accounts were remarkably similar. I will therefore quote Peter Akere verbatim and at some length, because I consider his story remarkable and illuminating and a paraphrase would do it less than justice:

> ... On 23rd April, 1968, Federal troops entered Ogoni Division (1963 population 231,000) at four different points--Bane and Kalaoko on the Imo River, Kaa on the Andoni River, and Bodo on the Bonny River. They swept the biafran troops before them, meeting resistance only at Nchia, some sixteen miles from Port Harcourt. Having broken through this defence they converged on Port Harcourt. Biafran resistance in the Ogoni sector was so poor that sooner than later, the field commanders who had undertaken this difficult assignment ran into very serious trouble with the rebel high command. Some faced the firing squad for alleged sabotage because Federal advance through the important oil- bearing area of Ogoni was too fast to be imagined. It appeared that they had not put up a fight at all. In their own defence these commanders alleged that the Ogoni people had collaborated with Federal troops, had shown the enemy various tracks which were unknown to biafran soldiers who, fearing lest they might be surrounded, had had to withdraw. No doubt, there were several Ogoni people who were only too eager to co-operate with the Federal troops (after all the Federal Administrator for Bonny, Mr K. B. Saro-Wiwa was an Ogoni) but the Federal troops could also have marched to Port Harcourt with minimum co-operation. Whatever the case, the story of the biafran field commanders was totally believed to our entire discredit as will be seen later.
>
> Port Harcourt finally fell on 17th May, 1968. Ogoni had, been liberated in less than three weeks. But what had happened to the civilian populace of Ogoni in those three weeks?
>
> Most of them had evacuated their towns. One or more of

unfortunate event.

The first explanation is psychological. The instinct of self-preservation is so strong in man that he is rarely willing to die. For instance, a family in the town of Bomu was not ready to leave, but a mortar shell killed two members of the family. This family was in no mood, after burying the dead, to debate. Goaded by the instinct of self-preservation, the survivors fled out of harm's way.

The next factor which contributed in some small measure towards the massive evacuation was the air-raids and the propaganda that followed each raid. The tremor which this bird of destruction sent down the spine of our people and many other people is beyond my powers of description. Like a vulture ready to pounce on a corpse it hovered at very low altitude "laying eggs" of very solid bullets. Biafran propagandists made much capital of it. They said that since the enemy's attempts by land and sea had failed, they were desperately making the last effort, this time by air, to perfect the genocide which was begun in May, 1966. They amplified this piece of propaganda by saying that if the Ogoni people were any exception to the projected wholesale massacre, their homes would not have been bombed. The air raids became so frequent in April that we were advised by members of the Civil Defence Corps to take cover in the bushes. Oftentimes, we sojourned far into the thick of the countryside to seek shelter. It became routine to set out to one's hiding place at dawn and return home a little after dusk. Thus established in this practice, most people easily fell prey to the information ordering them, at the approach of Federal troops, to evacuate their homes for a brief while in their own interest, while the soldiers prepared to meet the challenge which the ugly military situation had posed.

This third factor was responsible for most of the evacuation. The order to evacuate was immediately backed up with force and as men and women were evacuated in Government vans, army personnel were carefully and systematically supervising every inch of the evacuation to make sure that it was thorough and perfect. Most of the *people deserved to be enlightened on this unprecedented confusion, but were deceived into thinking that the exodus was simply an affair which would last for three days. This explains why some of them equipped themselves with only the barest necessities.*

A few fanatics and position seekers who had co-operated with the biafran regime also left, lest their complicity with the rebel soldier should earn them a Federal reprimand.

Having been forced to evacuate, some moved on to Port Harcourt, others stopped briefly around Ban-Ogoi and Ebubu. For some people, it was not a brief stop: it was a permanent stop and as the wave of battle swept past, leaving the immediate vicinity untouched, they went back to their homes and saw biafran propaganda collapsing under the weight of practical test. They were well received by the Federal troops. Other people moved on, unsuspecting of the great luck of their compatriots.

As there was no adequate transport arrangement very few benefitted from it; for the majority it was a great trek. At Rumuokwurusi, some took a path which led into the heart of Ikwerre County; others proceeded to St. John's College, Diobu where they were camped temporarily. In the meantime, three days had expired and with a poor and ill-organized rehabilitation set-up, the fate to come was seen in its proper perspective.

The first indication of biafran hostility was demonstrated on the Ogonis at St. John's, Diobu, when almost all males above fifteen years were taken away in several vehicles to concentration camps at Obike and Imerienwe where they were to await death pending confirmation of a rumour that the Ogonis were responsible for the successful invasion of their land by Federal forces. All others who remained at Diobu had to trek out of the place, one after the other, until the fall of Port Harcourt. Thus separated from the menfolk, the women trudged slowly, wearing a mournful look, through the thirty-five mile route between Port Harcourt and Elele. Some diverted their course into Choba and parts of Etche; some moved up to Ahoada, Edeoha, Omoku, Ogba County, or

Owerri; others converged around Elele while those who had taken the route through Aba settled in Ngwaland.

At first it was possible to win bread by engaging in petty trade but this was not a general case since only a few could raise capital for it. Some others were taken on hire by native inhabitants to work on their farms. The proceeds from the endeavour were not sufficient to keep body and soul together and our people began to die in such large numbers that the Roman Catholic priests had to step in with some relief materials. Not all benefitted from the scheme at its initial stage, of course; it was designed to be a palliative not the cure; an antidote not the panacea, to the problem of hunger. And it is estimated that between May and August, 1968, more than four thousand Ogonis died.

Another contributory factor to the high mortality was exposure; for those who could not be accommodated in make-shift huts stayed out and were exposed to the raw weather. Moreover it was rainy season. Hunger therefore combined with disease to create a situation in which life became not only intolerable but also useless. From this background, the humanitarians undertook action under the compulsion of a duty to save the refugees from disaster the imminence of which had been made inescapably clear to all.

The Kampala Peace Talks had ended in a fiasco as Sir Louis Mbanefo, biafra's Chief Negotiator, announced that he did not have a mandate to discuss surrender terms. With the resolution of "fighting to a finish", anxiety and nostalgia began to colour the refugee atmosphere as there appeared no limit in sight to their sufferings. The extent of the home sickness was epitomized in a choral composition by an Apostolic Pastor which ran thus: "If ever and when I get to my home, I will send most heartfelt songs of praise to God in high Heavens."

Pagans were converted and fallen Christians retraced their steps into the service of God hoping to go to heaven when they would meet the death that was staring them in the face. There were many and more cases of baptism while the sacraments of Matrimony and Holy Communion were lavishly administered to those who wanted them. Only a minority who had remembered to take their juju along but forgot their money behind persisted in their fetish practices. In the meantime what had happened to our brothers in detention at Imerienwe and Obike? Their charge was no mean one and if it could be further substantiated, they would all, it was alleged, be buried alive.

By the end of June, only eighteen of several hundred had escaped. Such was the seriousness of the situation that petitions began to rain on State House, Umuahia, from prominent Ogonis who were influential with the biafran government. The Efik Administrative Officer who was in charge of Ogoni Division also affirmed that the Ogonis were not saboteurs. The big argument that was raised was that the charge itself was trumpery as there was no evidence to back it up. Besides, if the mere fact of Federal success in Ogoni was sufficient to incriminate all her menfolk, why was the same view not taken of the males from other areas which fell into Federal hands long before?

They were all discharged in the first week of September, 1968 and when they came back they could not find enough words in which to narrate their weird experience...
***

By the end of September, 1968, Ogoni refugees were seen around Orlu, Umuahia, Ngwa and parts of Owerri Province including Ohaji farm settlement and Mbaise (in the Ibo heartland). Now that they had converged, it was possible for the Rehabilitation Commission to take a general census of refugees. The statistics, after the exercise, revealed a figure which put Ogoni on top of the list on a divisional basis.

We began to wonder if the same strictness and extreme thoroughness with which the biafrans supervised evacuation in Ogoni was employed in similar operations elsewhere. We were certain that Ogoni was not the most populous division in the former Eastern Nigeria. We knew that there were fewer biafran loyalists in Ogoni than in most of the areas which up till then had been liberated by Federal forces. In the light of these two reflections, what would account for this abnormal

rise in our population in war time? One of two things must
have happened. Either the Ibos had conducted the operation
in their own areas with inertia and unconcern knowing very
well that Federal soldiers were harmless to civilians. Or, they
presumed too much on the loyalty of their own people and so
were less vigilant over them during an invasion falsely hoping
that they would normally leave their homes. In either event,
they had played us a trick by forcing us at gun point to
evacuate our fertile land while they allowed their brothers the
discretion of evacuating. In which case, we were now being
held as hostages.

Now in the Ibo heartland, life became more difficult and
all the problems of refugees were heightened. The Divisional
Administrative Officers were charged with the duty of
re-settling these unfortunate persons and so they organized
them into little groups and sent them to live in school rooms
which were not yet occupied by the army. In some villages we
were well received while in others, the natives argued that
they had never before benefitted from the Eastern Nigerian
Government and so would not share with her the problem of
accommodating refugees. To strengthen their stand, they
further argued that they were loyal biafrans and therefore
were not prepared to harbour a people who were saboteurs in
the eyes of the government. The point, however, is that they
knew they were not self- sufficient agriculturally, and any
addition to their population would inevitably increase the
number dependent on the paltry resources then available.
Recognizing this, the Government dismissed their fears by
urging them to accommodate refugees as their upkeep was
entirely Government's responsibility.

We were then taken in but with the additional warning that
if we led in the enemy and caused them to evacuate their
homes, they would kill us, beginning from the oldest man to
the smallest child. It did not end there. At midnight, they
would surround our dwelling places, armed as they were, and
send in a small number to check (and pilfer) our belongings.
This, it was claimed, was a security measure taken in their
own interest to ensure that the strangers in their midst were

not Nigerian agents. The most surprising thing was that Ibos of all conditions took part in this exercise. Once, in Ngwaland, a former Federal Minister joined in the exercise. How they ever thought those starving women and children could be agents of the enemy, I can hardly understand. The fact, however, is that whether their impression was true or not, they did not care. They found the pretext a very convenient platform for carrying out their misdeeds. When the situation got unbearable, refugees resident in Aba Province sent a letter to the Provincial Administrator in Aba and got the following reply:

GOVERNMENT OF THE REPUBLIC OF BIAFRA

PROVINCIAL OFFICE, ABA
C/O N.N.C.C. P.O. BOX 47,
NBAWSI.

Our Ref: ABP/PA/EM/2
7th October, 1968

Ogoni Elements in Aba Province
c/o Mr. Pius Donu Kinako,
Ministry of Agric.
Nbawsi.

Sir,
AN APPEAL FOR HELP

I am in receipt of your very pathetic letter about the plight of Ogoni persons now refugees in Aba Province. Frankly, I am aware of the difficulties of my fellow Biafrans who by accident happen to inhabit a certain section of our country and discover the tribal name 'Ogoni'. I am constrained to think that the molestation has been monstrous in recent times.

I want you to believe me that as the Administrator, I have in the past (not in the press) been doing everything possible to minimize the suffering of these Biafrans. I have spoken at public places; I have threatened persons, areas and even army personnel. I have fumed and boiled and undertaken tours on account of this trouble. Unfortunately it had not quite succeeded to the extent that will attract my admiration. I have been labelled 'a saboteur' for championing the cause of the innocent Ogoni persons.

The whole thing stems from real ignorance which is one of our greatest setbacks in this war. Senior Army Officers have lost their lives because of the ignorance of the rank and file. At Ntigha my own Ngwa people drove away threateningly my own family for allegedly telephoning Lagos to come and bomb Ntigha - Ngwas of my own Province. Is this possible? It is crass ignorance!

So please ask your people to cheer up. It will soon be a thing of the past. I am doing my best which is now gathering momentum.

M. N. Onwuma (Signed)
Provincial Administrator, Aba Province

With the flight of time, our sufferings extracted much commiseration and sympathy from a few of them. I must therefore mention to their credit that some of them freely and generously dished out presents to those who were worst hit. I am myself exceedingly grateful to my personal friends, who at different times made considerable sacrifice to keep me alive.

There were several Ibos who had heard reports about Ogoni and how the land was abundant in plenty and they felt sorrowful for her children who had, by force of circumstance, become beggars. However, the hostile actions of the large majority dwarfed such considerations and kindnesses.

Government passed the responsibility for feeding us to the Rehabilitation Commission which administered the food flown in by rebel planes belonging to various humanitarian organizations. It has to be said that the Rehabilitation

Commission was not efficient in its administration of the food that was being flown in. There were two categories of displaced persons demanding different levels of treatment. There were those who had fled from disturbed areas to their very homes whilst on the other hand, there were those who fled from their own homes. The former were known as returnees while the latter were designated refugees. This second category merited special treatment and that is why the humanitarian organizations had voted sixty per cent of their total consignment of food for them, leaving forty per cent for the first group.

But by arrangement of the Rehabilitation Commission, the reverse became the case. Army officers had their own special share of anything that was brought in. Kwashiokor clinics and feeding centres were established ostensibly to drain into private hands the food that was assigned to refugees. This is evidenced by the frequent struggles by the Biafran Red Cross, the Akanu Ibiam National Ambulance and the St. John's Ambulance detachments in every village for supervision of these establishments. Worst of all, attendance at these institutions was the exclusive prerogative of the natives of the places where they were sited. It was only in Orlu and Umuahia Divisions that there was any exception to the rule.

Secondly, it was so arranged that appointments of refugee officials such as Directors, Storekeepers, Wardens, Welfare Officers and Security Officers fell on fellow Ibos, thus excluding the Ogonis from the policy-making body of their own camps. They would only elect two refugee representatives to serve on the Camp Management Committee which comprised the officials and three "responsible" persons from the village. They then swooped on relief food, articles of clothing and money and diverted as much as pleased them to private use, not minding the plight of those for whom those things were intended. The most lucrative appointment then was Camp Director and it most lucrative appointment then was Camp Director and it was only given to the highest bidder. Once appointed, he would normally hasten to recover the money spent on obtaining his post.

The first attempt at misappropriation of relief food was organized at Camp level through a scheme of central cooking. By this method, the food for the general refugee group in a particular camp would be cooked together and then served out to them individually. It was as if refugees could not cook their own food. Apart from the inherent disadvantages in bulk preparation, it was noticed that far less than the stipulated quantity

of any item was used at all. Whatever remained was not accounted for. The system was abolished after refugees had shown their resentment by boycotting the meals.

The next resort was to serve out dry ration to refugees so that they could prepare their own food for themselves, considering their individual tastes. When it is realised that these officials were expected to feed from the refugee store as an additional allowance to the salaries they were paid from their original places of work, one can imagine fully the feelings of justification with which the dishonest ones abused their position. Any one who rebelled against their authority was conscripted into the army. And so corrupt practice remained unfettered and unchecked.

At this time, the value of money was fast declining and money no longer served as a store of value. The refugees were benefiting only on the smallest scale imaginable from the relief supplies. Employment was out of the question and the only one which was available locally, though not always, was labour on the farms. But the cost of hire was seriously depreciating. Apart from that, nine cases of murder of Ogoni labourers had only recently been recorded. They had been tricked to the farm under the pretext of hire and were eventually decapitated and cannibalized. After these ghastly incidents, most of our people developed a cold attitude over accepting any offer of hire which was their last hope of working for pay. The lucky ones who were able to take some clothes from home next embarked on selling their clothes. But how many clothes did they possess and how many of these were marketable?

Those who had any deposit with the banks could travel to the towns where they were temporarily located and receive a maximum payment of five pounds per week. But transport was an acute problem in biafra and cost of travel to the bank would in a majority of cases exceed the withdrawal to be authorized by the Manager. Also, there were occasions when customers were not paid any money because there was none. It would therefore amount to spending the little one had on transport and returning empty- handed. And the exigency of the times in which we lived was such that any picnic of that nature was not only a luxury but could be equated with suicide.

Another potent obstacle to any travel was the fact that one had to restrict one's movements because of dangers on the way. Reverses on the side of biafra had become so notable, in spite of the mountains of propaganda which were piled from the Ministry of Information, that enlistment into the army was no longer volunteered except by a very small number who preferred death on the battle field to death by hunger. Now, if the war was to continue (and certainly it had to because it had not yet reached the stage where Sir Francis Ibiam hoped that "even the grass will fight," then soldiers had to be recruited to fill the numerous and progressively increasing vacancies at the fronts. Little wonder then that conscription became the order of the day and hence the danger to civilian travellers.

A contributory factor toward conscription was the awareness on the part of rebel soldiers themselves that ill-equipped, rag-tag, hungry and unpaid as they were, biafra was not worth fighting for. Initially, it was possible to resist "police action" with machetes and hope to return with "ten Hausa heads". But with the declaration of total war, and in the face of an army which, realizing the folly of its past mistakes of softness, was determined, fortified with every material and moral encouragement, to crush the rebellion, it became unthinkable to regard battle as a wrestling match which one could engage in without arms.

Conscious of the fact that they were being used as cannon fodder, painfully reminiscent of the second fact that their efforts were not remunerated and fully aware that they were always on the retreat during nearly every campaign as a result of which there was no future in their struggles, the rebel soldiers employed an idea styled "No. 6". The idea was that self-preservation must take precedence over biafran survival and not the latter over the former as had been the case. Consequently they straggled from their various duty posts at the fronts and even from the offices in the rear. It became so widespread that it was noticed in the Personnel Department, Statistics Division of the Army Headquarters that there were more soldiers on paper than were available for deployment. In order to remedy this deficiency, conscription was endorsed as a main recruitment policy.

Originally, it was intended to affect only able-bodied males who were not engaged in essential services. These were defined to include all civil servants, company employees, staff of the various Directorates, humanitarian workers, religious clerks and those whose duties had any connection, no matter how remote, with the army. But very soon, practically every biafran, with the collaboration of those in authority, found himself accommodated in any of the above categories and so exempted from compulsory military service. The reaction of the government to this chicanery showed that it was too clever to be cheated.

Most civil servants were declared redundant and deployed to fight for the nation. Only bank officials, pastors *and staff of Research and Production units were really exempted. The Ministry that was maliciously attacked was the Ministry of Agriculture which had resolved itself into the Food Production Directorate. The reason is that agriculture, which from time immemorial, has always thrived under conditions of settled life, did not, consequent upon the social and economic dislocation caused by the war, find such favourable condition. As a result no food was produced and so, since the Directorate was not living up to expectation, their workers were the constant targets of conscriptors. The other government departments were ordered to retain a skeletal staff to run essential services and most of the junior staff were recruited into the army.*

How did this new policy affect the Ogonis? It was easy for those who were still in their own homes to hide as a means of evading conscription. But for a people whose dwelling-place was exposed outright and whose names, sex, age and other details were all in the camp register, where would they run to? To add insult to injury, most camp directors saw in conscription an opportunity to eliminate over-inquisitive refugees who hankered after every detail of what food was brought in, what was rationed and what remained. Some of them therefore willingly submitted lists of Ogoni youths in their camps to military authorities who traced them out and sent them to the Training Depots from where they never returned. Life became a burden for young men who no longer felt safe and had to take cover during the day in 'bunkers' which they dug in nearby bushes. When this device was known, the camps were surrounded by night and raided by conscriptors. Large numbers were often carried away in night operations.

Recognizing the problem which illiteracy would pose to the use of English as the medium of instruction in the Military schools, the Government so organized it that different vernaculars were used. This was calculated to guard against any complaint of academic disqualification in the event of conscription. It is not then surprising that in only three months of operation, Ogoni had formed a Task Force. Very soon however, it was dissolved out of tribal fears and the boys were distributed among the brigades under the 12th Division. Since most of them were not educated to take up jobs as clerks or tradesmen, they found themselves at the very first line of battle. Mortality rate was high, alarmingly high and yet there was no remedy.

And in the camps, our people were dying at the rate of eight, sometimes, ten in a week, in the larger camps. They died of hunger; they died of disease; they died of exhaustion; above all, they died of despair.

***

This story corroborates N. U. Akpan's assertions and confirms the horrendous experience which the Ogoni suffered during the civil war for no other reason than that they live on oil-bearing land, are a minority, and are therefore ready candidates for genocide. The Federal troops did not treat the Ogoni whom they found badly but the Federal Government had other plans for their gradual despoliation and eventual extermination.

An estimated thirty thousand Ogonis (or over ten per cent of the ethnic group) died in the war. When my book was published twenty-one years after the end of the war and this fact was released for the first time to the Nigerian public, it made no impression whatsoever on Nigerian officials or people.

The only conclusion that can be drawn therefrom is that the Ogoni live in a nation which is determined to exterminate them and that Ogoni lives mean nothing whatsoever to Nigeria and other Nigerians, and, I dare to add, the murderous country would be pleased to see Ogoni territory rid of all its inhabitants so that its oil resources can fall freely into "Nigerian" hands.

If I ever harboured any doubt about that, what happened in Ogoni shortly after the cessation of hostilities put paid to all such doubt.

CHAPTER 5

THE SHELL-B.P. ROLE

Ever before the defeat of biafra on the battlefield, the Shell-B.P. Company had recommenced its mining operations in Ogoni. The Federal Government needed the proceeds from oil to prosecute the war in its incompetent, wasteful, devious manner. Consequently, every encouragement was given to Shell-B.P. to continue its genocidal plans against the Ogoni people.

It has to be said that at that time, the Nigerian government knew pretty little of the oil industry. There were not enough trained men in the relevant supervising Ministries of the Government to draft the laws and regulations which would bind Shell-B.P. to minimum standards of civilized behaviour.

Shell-BP consequently seized upon this fact and displayed the ugliest possible face of international capitalism. Operating among a peasant population which, as this study has shown, knew little of the ways of the modern world, Shell-B.P. has behaved cruelly, stupidly and in a racist manner.

Over the years, right from 1958, the Ogoni people have been engaged in a no-win war with Shell-B.P. Matters came to a head in April 1970 when Ogoni leaders, unable to bear the chicanery and heartlessness of the Company, were forced to petition the Military Governor of Rivers State in a carefully considered memorandum. At that time, I was a Commissioner (Minister) with responsibility for education in the State and was sent a copy of the petition for my information. The petition, reproduced hereunder, speaks for itself as does the reaction of Shell-B.P. to it.

> *Ogoni Divisional Committee,*
> *c/o Chief T. N. Adda-Kobani,*
> *12 Victoria Street,*
> *Port Harcourt.*
> *25th April, 1970.*

His Excellency the Military Governor,
Rivers State of Nigeria,

Port Harcourt.

Your Excellency,

HUMBLE PETITION OF COMPLAINT ON SHELL-BP OPERATIONS IN OGONI DIVISION

May it please Your Excellency to give your fatherly attention and sympathetic consideration to the complaints of your people of Ogoni Division who have suffered in silence as a direct result of the discovery and exploitation of mineral oil and gas in this Division over the past decades.

2. While it is a fact of history that the petroleum oil industry has given the national economy of Nigeria a great leap forward, it is equally and sadly true that neither the nation nor the Shell-BP Company has ever given serious and deserved consideration to the effects which this industry has had, and will continue to have, on the economy and life of the people of this Division, which has become the main home of the oil industry in Nigeria.

3. In addition to the Refinery which is located at Alesa, the Bomu, Bodo-West, Korokoro and Ebubu oil fields which are among the nation's most extensive and most productive oil-fields are also sited in Ogoni Division. Besides these production wells, several other wells will soon go into production in all other parts of the Division.

4. Land is a very rare commodity in the Rivers State, and even more so in Ogoni Division. Ogoni Division contains one of the highest population concentrations in Nigeria, rising from a density of over 500 per square mile in Eleme to 1,200 per square mile in the Gokana area, the home of the vast Bomu oil-fields. It is in view of this that we are alerting the State Government to the fact that the Shell-BP operations in this Division are seriously threatening the well-being, and even the very lives of the people of Ogoni Division.

5. About two decades ago, agriculture was the mainstay of the economy of Ogoni Division. But to-day, the entire economy of our people has been completely disrupted through the connivance of a nation which seems to have allowed the Shell-BP, a purely commercial organization, to enter upon and seize the people's land at will. So long as the nation gets her royalties, nobody bothers what happens to the poor rural farmer whose land has been expropriated. Here our delta-type alluvial soil possesses a high degree of fertility, and each acre yields an average of £1,000 (one thousand pounds) to £2,000 (two thousand pounds) per farming season to its cultivator. But without negotiation, the nation allows a land-grabbing commercial company to seize large stretches of rich agricultural lands, paying a scandalously meagre once-and-for-all £1:10/-per acre. Deprived thus of his only source of income, the dispossessed farmer is ruined, and his children can no longer obtain an education nor his family a decent life.

6. In the same way, the Shell-BP destroys cash crops and economic trees without giving adequate compensation to their owners. A few weeks ago, caterpillars of the Shell-BP entered into cultivated farms in the Bomu area and mercilessly ploughed down acres and acres of cultivated crops; yams, maize, pepper, melons, fluted pumpkins, cassava, okro, garden eggs, and other valuable crops in flagrant violation of Section 17, Sub-sections (b) v and (c) ii of the Petroleum (Drilling and Production) Regulations, 1969. Your Excellency, the attached photographs of this atrocity speak for themselves. Because the Shell-BP knows too well that none of the poor villagers being dispossessed has ever had the benefit of reading these Petroleum Regulations, or of even knowing of their existence, the company does not bother to consult them. What Your Excellency sees in these photographs is a picture of what is happening to our people everywhere in our Division where-ever the Shell-BP operates: Korokoro, Ebubu, Kpean etc. It is all the more distressing to note that the victims of these caterpillar raids are poor returnees (from the war) whom we have encouraged to till the soil in order to raise a paltry subsistence. Your Excellency will agree that for such poor people, the war will never end since the hard realities of the war are still with them today.

7. When Your Excellency recently honoured this Division with an extensive tour, you were shown large acres of mangrove swamps that have been destroyed by the periodic out-flow of crude oil into our rivers and streams, which have killed off not only mangrove trees, but fishes and crabs, mudskippers, oysters, shell-fishes, etc. on which the livelihood of the poorer people depends. In this way, our rights under Section 23 of the Petroleum (Drilling and Production) Regulations, 1969, have been violated with impunity by the Shell-BP.

8. A few years ago, our streams were blessed with pure and sparkling water. But in the Gokana area of the Division, most inland waters, rivers and water courses have today been polluted by crude oil, mud and other fluids which have contaminated our water supply in contravention of Section 25 of the Petroleum (Drilling and Production) Regulations, 1969. And yet, all entreaties made to the Shell-BP to provide the people with alternative water-supply have been rebuffed. Our people have been compelled to sacrifice all life-supporting necessities so that the nation may enjoy economic boom from the oil industry.

9. Before the Shell-BP began to prospect for oil in Ogoni Division our untarred roads were in very motorable condition, thanks to our firm and well-drained soil. But twenty years of hard use by the company's heavy vehicles, some of them ranging between twenty to thirty-two tons in weight, has broken the resistance of these roads, thereby making them unmotorable for most of the rainy season. When our people have requested for a few coats of tar on these roads, the Shell-BP have often told us that road maintenance and repairs are the responsibility of the State Government.

10. Your Excellency, neither from the Shell-BP nor from the successive Governments have we received the slightest consideration in the widespread destitution that has been our sad lot as a direct result of the oil industry in Ogoni Division. The uprooted and displaced farmers are left without alternative means of subsistence. No special consideration was ever given to the employment of our people in the services of the company. There is only one single son of Ogoni Division on the Senior Staff of the Shell-BP and there are less than a dozen in the junior staff segment. Today there is similarly only one Ogoni son in the Administrative Class of the State Government Service. In the award of Government and Shell-BP Scholarships, no special notice has been taken of the fact that the education of our youth has suffered tremendous disabilities from the reduction in the earning capacity of our people.

11. The current Petroleum (Drilling and Production) Regulations of 1969 still suffers from the immoral political thinking of the First Republic. It is a sad irony of our history that none of the areas providing this greatest source of our national wealth has ever had the privilege of having a strong voice in the processes of law-making in this country. The result has always been that no attention has ever been paid to the fate of the poor people who bear the full weight of the national economic burden on their backs.

12. Your Excellency, we are crying to you for sympathy because we have these recent years been victims of a callous neglect by successive Governments whose only interests are the royalties which accrue to them every year from the oil companies. The people of Ogoni Division are informing all men of reason who have a conscience that the millions of pounds which the Shell-BP constantly pays to our Government is blood-money, extracted from the very veins of our dying people. We are respectfully requesting Your Excellency and the Government which you so honourably head to disburden your conscience of this conspiracy against our people.

13. In view of the foregoing, the people of Ogoni Division are seeking the fraternal assistance of Your Excellency's Government in alleviating the suffering of your people of this Division. We lent our support and energy to the struggle for the creation of the Rivers State in a united Nigeria because we have always believed that we can obtain justice only at the hands of our own brothers who were our companions in suffering in the First Republic.

14. We are respectfully requesting the Rivers State Government to help in the revision of the Petroleum laws in a way that will give some consideration to the fact that the nation has been collecting her fabulous oil royalties on the ruin and destitution of a section of her population.

15. We request that in any event, negotiation for the acquisition of land not owned by Government should be a bilateral transaction between the land-owner and the prospecting company, with the State Government sitting in as arbitrator. This happens in other oil-producing countries and can happen here.

16. We request that no less than £1,000 (one thousand pounds) be paid to land owners as rents per acre per annum for land acquired for oil exploitation and production.

17. We submit that where a people's water supply has been polluted and contaminated, or any of their life-supporting necessities destroyed as a direct result of oil exploration or production, it should be recognized that the company has an obligation to make alternative arrangements to supply these needs.

18. We are calling on the conscience of our dear countrymen to recognize that a people who have lost their sources of livelihood in the process of enriching the nation, deserve greater consideration by the country and the commercial company which is tapping this wealth, in the award of scholarships, in greater employment opportunities and in the award of contracts.

19. We refer again to paragraph 6 and to the photographs of wilful destruction attached hereto, and request that a special and immediate rehabilitation programme be arranged to resettle these poor returnee farmers who were recently deprived of their farms, their crops, their labour and virtually their lives, by the Shell-BP. Substantial sums of money should be laid out to enable them establish meaningful business. Having now been uprooted from their only sources of obtaining a decent living, alternative opportunities should be created for them now in the award of Government and Shell-BP contracts, in Government and Company employment, and in the award of special scholarships to their children in school, in college and University.

20. The people of Ogoni Division confidently believe that their State Government exists to protect their lives, property and material well-being against political or economic oppression and exploitation.

21. We shall feel highly honoured if Your Excellency can grant a delegation of the people of Ogoni Division the favour of an interview at your earliest convenience.

We humbly remain,
Your Excellency's most loyal people.

Sgd. 1. Chief W.Z.P. Nzidee 2. F.O.L. Yowika 3. N.A. Ndegwe
4. E.N. Kobani 5. O.B. Nalelo 6. Chief A.O. Ngei 7. Obo Ngofa
ON BEHALF OF OURSELVES AND THE ENTIRE PEOPLE OF OGONI DIVISION IN THE RIVERS STATE OF NIGERIA.
Copy:-
  The Federal Commissioner for Mines and Power,
  Federal Ministry of Mines and Power, Lagos.

  The Chief Petroleum Engineer,
  Federal Ministry of Mines and Power, Lagos.

  The Managing Director,

Shell-BP Petroleum Development Co. Ltd., Lagos.

The Commissioner,
Ministry of Agriculture, Fisheries and Natural Resources,
Rivers State of Nigeria, Port Harcourt.

Mr K. B. Tsaro-Wiwa,
Commissioner for Education, Rivers State, Port Harcourt.

Mr O. O. Ngei,
Commissioner for Works, Land and Transport,
Rivers State. Port Harcourt.

The Head of Operation,
Shell-BP, Port Harcourt.

A little over two months later, Shell-B. P. replied as follows:

H.E. The Military Governor,
Rivers State,
PORT HARCOURT.

Your Excellency,

OIL OPERATIONS IN OGONI DIVISION.

We refer to the "HUMBLE PETITION OF COMPLAINT FROM SHELL-BP OPERATIONS IN OGONI DIVISION", dated 25th April, 1970, addressed to Your Excellency by the "Ogoni Divisional Commission" and copied the Federal Commissioner for Mines and Power, and the Rivers State Civil Commissioners. This petition is one of a series which have originated in Ogoni Division over the past few years attempting to place development and other responsibilities on this Company which can only properly be undertaken by Government or by a Government agency. In support of such contentions, statements are usually made which, on examination, bear little relation to what is actually taking place. Regrettably, this petition is no exception to the rule and we deal with the various matters raised in it in detail in the appendix to this letter.

As you know, the main aim and purpose of an oil Company must be to find and produce hydrocarbons as efficiently as possible. This is the area in which it makes a very significant contribution to the overall economic development of any country in which it operates. As is the case with the other oil Companies operating in Nigeria our obligations and responsibilities are clearly delineated in the agreements made with the Federal Government and by the Laws and Regulations relating to the oil industry in Nigeria. These have always been meticulously observed by this Company. We have, however been extremely careful to ensure that our operations cause minimal disturbance to the people in the areas in which we operate and we think that this clearly emerges from the content of the attached appendix.

As with any special pleading, the petition exaggerates or misrepresents in one direction (e.g. the amount of land occupied for oil operations in Ogoni Division) and minimizes in the other (e.g. the amount of compensation paid by Shell-BP in Ogoni Division over the past years). There can be no doubt, however, that the incidental benefits accruing to Ogoni Division from Shell-BP's presence there greatly outweighs any disadvantages.

We have given very careful consideration to the advisability of writing to you on this matter and have finally concluded that the inaccuracies in the petition should not remain unanswered. We are sending copies of the letter to the Governor and Commissioners of the Rivers State who received copies of the petition.

Yours faithfully,
for: SHELL-BP PETROLEUM DEVELOPMENT
COMPANY OF NIGERIA LIMITED.

(Sgd.) J. SPINKS
MANAGER, EASTERN OPERATIONS.

APPENDIX TO LETTER NO.PUB/2110 DATED 9/6/70

AND ADDRESSED TO THE CHIEF PETROLEUM ENGINEER
MINISTRY OF MINES & POWER, LAGOS.
OIL OPERATIONS IN OGONI DIVISION

The drilling location to which the petition refers, although difficult to identify from the photograph accompanying the petition which could relate to clearing for any construction project in Rivers State, is probably BOMU VNOM 1.

The total amount of land occupied for this location and access road was just over 7 acres (7.372).

The total amount of compensation paid in respect of surface rights (i.e. economic crops & trees) was £1,266.8.7d.

In addition an annual rental at the rate of £4 per acre per annum was paid and will be paid in future years.

Compensation was paid to land and crop owners on 29th Jan. 1970.

The signatories for the land numbered 9 and 181 persons received compensation in respect of surface rights.

There have been no complaints to us from the actual land owners or crop owners from the time negotiations commenced until the present time.

Comments directly related to specific inaccuracies in the Petition are given below. The paragraph numbering of the Petition is used:

Paragraph 2

It is a continuing misconception held in Ogoni Division that the "main home of the oil industry in Nigeria" is Ogoni Division.
This is not the case. About 15% of the crude oil produced by Shell-BP in Nigeria originates from Ogoni Division and Ogoni produced crude forms a smaller proportion of total Nigeria crude oil production. Shell-BP has, however, always been aware that certain special problems, quite unrelated to oil operations, do exist in Ogoni Division and as is witnessed by its inauguration and financing in 1966 of the Ogoni Rural Community Project has attempted to make a significant contribution towards resolving them.

Paragraph 4

The 1963 census showed the population in Ogoni Division to average out at about 564 persons per square mile. This gives a population density of less than one person per acre.

Paragraph 5

The approximate total area of land comprised in Ogoni Division is 264,320 acres. Shell-BP occupies less than 1,000 acres of land for all its oil operations in Ogoni. This is just over a third of one percent of the total land area (.378%). This illustrates that the statement "the entire economy of our people has been completely disrupted etc.", is untenable.

The contention that "each acre yields an average of £1,000-£2000 (one thousand to two thousand pounds) per farming season" is a remarkable exaggeration which bears no relationship to the value of agricultural yields in Ogoni as any Government Agricultural Officer would confirm. It is also in direct contradiction with the statement in paragraph 6 that only "a paltry subsistence" can be raised from the soil. It is of interest in this connection that the well-known champion of Ogoni rights, Mr. K. B. Tsaro-Wiwa, in his recent pamphlet "The Ogoni Nationality Today and Tomorrow" states that the cash income in Ogoni has been estimated at £30 to £40 (thirty to forty pounds) per year per family.

The allegation that landowners are paid "a scandalously meagre once-and-for-all £1.10. (one pound, ten shilling) per acre" has no foundation in fact. In addition to surface rights compensation (see above, £1,266.8.7 in the case of local Bomu VNOM) an annual rental is paid. The rates of these annual rentals are approved by Government and have over the years been raised by the Company on its own initiative. For example, the rental for dry farm land has been increased by 166% during the past six years. Current rentals are as follows:

    (a) Dry Farm Land per acre 80/-
    (b) Seasonal Swamp "   "   40/-
    (c) Swamp   "   "   20/-.

Paragraph 6

The quite foundationless statement that Shell-BP destroys valuable cash crops and economic trees without giving adequate compensation to their owners has been answered above.

Entry to work in the location area was approved by the Government representative after due consultation and after the above-mentioned compensation has been paid and was not in contravention of any of the provisions of Section 17 of the Petroleum (Production and Drilling) Regulations, 1969, including sub-sections (b)v and (c)ii. It is worth noting here that whenever possible in addition to receiving compensation at full rates, landowners are permitted to harvest mature crops.

Paragraph 7

As a result of military operations during the recent war certain oil installations were damaged and escapes of crude oil occurred. This can in no way be attributed to the acts of this Company which ceased operations in the former Eastern Region in August 1967 and did not re-enter Ogoni until late 1968 when its first acts were to prevent further spillages and to minimize the effects of those which had already taken place. The statement that the rights of the people "have been violated with impunity by the Shell-BP" again has no foundation in fact and the whole of the paragraph attempts to make the Company responsible for the effects of the war.

Paragraph 8

The comments given above regarding pollution apply equally to any streams and rivers affected by escapes of crude. This does not affect a wide area, however, and is a temporary, not permanent, condition. Again an exaggerated argument is being used in an attempt to influence the Company to undertake activities (i.e. the provision of an alternative water supply, presumably by drilling water wells) which do not lie within its province or responsibilities.

Paragraph 9

No non-Government organization can accept responsibility for general road development but where it can be clearly shown that the deterioration in any road is due exclusively to use by Company traffic, the Company will take corrective measures and this has happened on many occasions in the years we have been operating in Ogoni Division. It has also, on occasion, voluntarily improved the road system to the benefit of the whole community. As examples of such work done in the past we quote the following:

(a)   *Egberu-Kpopis Road (approx.7 miles)* - General widening, draining and tarring of about half a mile of the distance. One permanent bridge constructed.

(b)   *Kpopi-Bodo Road (approx. 5 miles)* · General widening, draining and reinforcing with laterite. Three permanent culverts built.

(c)   *Dere-Chara Road (approx. 5 miles)* - General widening and draining work. Two permanent bridges constructed.

(d)   *Bori-Kono Road* - There were four Company Bailey bridges on the road prior to the construction of permanent Government bridges.

(e)   *New Roads* - Shell-BP have built more than 20 miles of new roads connecting the drilling locations in the Division.

Paragraph 10

It is extremely improbable that there has been widespread destitution in Ogoni Division as a direct result of the oil industry in view of the proportionately very small area of land occupied by the oil industry and if farmers have indeed been uprooted, displaced and left without alternative means of subsistence it is indeed strange that there have been no such authenticated cases in the years in which we have been operating in Ogoni Division and that those alleged to have been treated in this way have complained neither to the appropriate Government representatives nor to this Company.

The inhabitants of Ogoni Division have been expected to qualify for employment and scholarships on the same basis as other Nigerian nationals. 39 persons from Ogoni are employed by this Company at the present time in various categories and capacities.

With regard to scholarship awards, the position is as follows:

(a)   We operate three types of scholarship schemes; University awards, Higher School Certificate and secondary school awards. The selection of candidates for our University awards, which are mostly for Engineering Courses, must obtain Higher School Certificate passes at Principal level "C" in Physics, Applied Mathematics and Pure Mathematics or in these subjects at the advanced level in the G.C.E.

(b)   The Higher School Certificate awards are made on the basis of our school programme. From talks and films given all the secondary schools in the operational areas, candidates are examined on the elementary aspects of the oil industry and the very best are selected for the awards. We have not however restarted this programme in the Eastern States as yet.

(c)   The secondary school awards are confined to children from our areas of operation and we have twenty such awards to children from Ogoni Division, and three of these were made in December 1969. It might perhaps be mentioned also in 1969 we made an Overseas University award to a boy from Ogoni even though he had only a West African School Certificate.

Paragraphs 15, 16, 17 and 19

The demands made in these paragraphs are in themselves intrinsically unrealistic and supported moreover by conclusions themselves based upon facts and premises which are patently incorrect. These misconceptions are tenacious and deeply rooted and the Company is willing to participate in any information programme which the Federal Government and the Rivers State Government may wish to mount in Ogoni Division.

I met Mr Spinks on one or two occasions while he was Manager, Eastern Operations of Shell-B.P. He struck me as a genial and accommodating man who was distressed by the terrible and unspeakable degradation of the Ogoni people and who would have loved to do something about it. The letter which he signed and circulated was a load of Shellspeak and I would doubt that he masterminded it. Like many other employees of Shell-B.P., he may have been the unwitting victim of a Satanic octopus which demands men's souls in return for cash and security. I would like to know if he lasted long in Shell-B.P. and what he may have done when he got transferred out of Port Harcourt after his letter had been written.

Shell's reply can be easily dismissed. A British Company which, as the letter indicates, does violence to the English language would gladly murder "foreign" peasants without compensation. So blind is the Company, it does not know the difference between a "Commission" and a "Committee". Efficiency in finding and producing hydrocarbons must mean in Shellspeak, the speedy extermination of human beings and their environment, particularly if these happen to be in Africa. Shell expects illiterate peasants to be the only ones who should protest against genocide by an organization which has the financial muscle to hire the best legal and other brains and which has wide experience in dealing with governments in various coasts and climes. Shell is not ashamed to mention the pittance it pays for valuable land and its complicity with the ethnic majority in Nigeria who have framed the laws which destroy the powerless minorities. Having polluted streams, Shell cannot see the need for providing alternative sources which are well within its means. For, before oil is ever struck, water is found. So why should the provision of water be such a problem for Shell? The Company must be cruel and sadistic. The number of Ogoni people whom the Company proudly advertises itself to have employed must make anyone but Shell laugh. The world would like to know whatever happened to the Ogoni Rural Community Project. How much did Shell spend on it? How much of that money ended up in the pockets of Shell employees and how much was actually expended on the project? What tax remission did Shell get for embarking on this dubious project? What are the "special problems" of the Ogoni which Shell professes to know? What did it do about them? Did those problems assist Shell to "find and produce hydrocarbons efficiently"? Did Shell therefore promote the "special problems" in its own self-interest while pretending to be contributing "towards resolving them"? The prodigious road-building capabilities of Shell are in full display even today in Ogoni. The Company could not possibly realize that making roads to "connect its drilling locations" is a serious disturbance to its hapless landlords. The peasant farmers are thereby forced to wear shoes which they cannot afford to their farms. This Company's antics make me sick.

A few days after this disgusting letter was received in government circles, the sins of Shell-B.P. and the deep and mortal wounds the Company has inflicted on the Ogoni people were shown up by its acts of omission. There was a major blow-out at the Bomu oilfield.

Coming at the end of a horrendous civil war which had brutalized the Ogoni people and hastened them on the path of extinction, the oil-blow out, which occurred towards the end of July 1970, showed up the insensitivity of the Company to human suffering and its complicity in the genocide of the Ogoni.

The first reactions to the blow-out came from the young people of Dere, the Ogoni village in which Shell had first struck oil in 1958:

A STATE OF EMERGENCY EXISTS TODAY
IN DERE - OGONI, RIVERS STATE
28th JULY, 1970

It has always been our view that the oil in Nigeria does not benefit landowners because the oil is found mainly in Minority Areas. The situation in Dere today goes to support the view, for what is happening here today could never have gone un-heard of as it is now, had it happened in the home of one of the majority groups in the country.

We in Dere today are facing a situation which can only be compared with our experiences during the civil war. This village of no less than 20,000 inhabitants produces the greatest oilfield this country has - BOMU, SHELL-BP chooses to call it for reasons best known to that Shylock of a company. It is nearly two weeks now when suddenly we were hinted that there was an explosion on this oilfield and that people should be on their alert. This 'revelation' came casually, perhaps secretly, from some friends who are employees of the company. Since then an ocean of crude oil had emerged, moving swiftly like a great river in flood, successfully swallowing up anything that comes on its way. These include cassava farms, yams, palms, streams, animals etc etc for miles on end. There is no pipeborne water and yet the streams, the only source of drinking water is coated with oil. You cannot collect a bucket of rain water for the roofs, trees and grass are all covered with oil. Anything spread outside in the neighbourhood is soaked with oil as the wind carries the oil miles away from the scene of the incident. Nor can you enter a bush without being soaked to the skin. People are barred from entering the farmlands for fear that they would carry naked lights. But the explosion is now in flames. Thrice during the Civil war the flow station was bombed setting the whole place on fire. It blazed so much that it was impossible to live in and around the village. Now a worse fire is blazing not quite a quarter of a mile from the village. The force of the explosion intermittently shades the whole land and sets buildings rocking. The fear that the houses would collapse any moment would not let the people sleep. They just keep awake at nights expecting the worst at any moment, nor can they move to farm to look for what to eat. But men and women forced by hunger "steal" occasionally into the 'ocean', some have to dive deep in oil to uproot already rotten yams and cassava. I am not a scientist to analyze what effects the breathing of dangerous gases the crude oil contains would have on the people, but suffice it to say that the air is polluted and smells only of crude oil. We are thus faced with a situation where we have no food to eat, no water to drink, no homes to live and worst of it all, no air to breathe. We now live in what Hobbes may describe as a STATE OF NATURE - a state where peace or security does not exist "... and the life of man is solitary, poor, nasty, brutish and short. "

Ogoni villagers drink water from polluted streams.

Oil pipelines on agricultural land in Ogoni.

Ecological change. Nypa palms displace mangrove trees.

Gas flares twenty-four hours a day.

Shell BP is the Leviathan to whom we have been forced to surrender all our Rights including our very LIFE. What is the company's answer to all our ills - to keep the emergency situation as dark as possible from the public. As a free born of Dere, and hearing of the situation, I came home to see things for myself, but I am not allowed entry into the area of disaster. Some great and well meaning sons of Ogoni have had the same bitter experience.

The situation in Dere today calls for sympathy from Shell BP, from the governments of the Federation, from the press and radio and from charitable organizations. We were among the worst sufferers in the then rebel held areas. For several days bombing was concentrated on us. The town was evacuated almost to a man by the rebels. Fortunately many returned between last December and January and started immediately to plant various crops on any available lands - crops that had now been completely destroyed by a stream of crude oil.

We have expected that by now helicopters of Government officials would be hovering over the area; that radios and the press would make the Dere emergency situation news items and commentaries. Yes, these have not been possible for after all, only a minute minority of the people of Nigeria live in Ogoni and much less in Dere. Our forefathers committed no crimes to have founded a home on top of the country's greatest source of wealth - wealth from which we derive no atom of benefit.

As I write the thought of it makes me sob for as I look around I remember the old ballad.

> The towns go down; the land decays ...
> Poor folk for bread, cry and weep.
> The mournful peasant leads his humble band,
> And while he sinks, without one arm to save,
> The country blooms - a garden and a grave

Five years ago a great son of Ogoni made this appeal to Shell BP, an appeal which is even more appropriate today than our good old days of 1965 by 1970 standard.

"Today, we need education, we need employment, we want to eat, we want to live. We do not want our children to remain out of school ... we do not want to lack money because Shell has removed land which used to be *our main source of revenue. In short, we do not want to live in a vicious circle in which we shall see the Shell BP as the authors of our misfortune and our oppressors ... Is it not an irony that those who live on top of wealth should be the poorest people in the nation? Shell BP can rectify this irony NOW if it wants to, AND IT SHOULD."*

And I add, well meaning Nigerians! Come over to Ogoni and help us!

SAM BADILO BAKO
SECONDARY/COMMERCIAL SCHOOL, TAABAA, OGONI, VIA PORT-HARCOURT.

Copy to:
1. *The News Editor, Radio Nigeria, Lagos.*
2. *The News Editor, Radio Television, Kaduna.*
3. *The Editor, Daily Times of Nigeria, Lagos.*
4. *The News Editor, Radio Nigeria, Port Harcourt.*

A PROTEST PRESENTED TO REPRESENTATIVES OF THE SHELL-BP DEV. CO. OF NIG. LTD. BY THE DERE YOUTHS ASSOCIATION. AGAINST THE COMPANY'S LACK OF INTEREST IN THE SUFFERINGS OF DERE PEOPLE WHICH SUFFERINGS ARE CAUSED AS A RESULT OF THE COMPANY'S OPERATIONS.

Sir,
    We the Youths of Dere (misnomered Bomu) are proud to be associated with the gigantic progress made by your Company since it started explorations in Nigeria. We are also impressed by the remarkable contribution she is making for the economic stability of Nigeria. You would candidly agree with us that DERE is a partner on this stage of progress, though in a varying and yet a conspicuous degree.
    But it is a great source of disappointment to us, to note that the Shell-BP is deliberately pursuing a Godless economic policy in our locality, an inhuman profiteering at the expense of our lives, whereby it sucks the liquid gold from our land but takes no interest in our welfare. The Company only contented on pleasing the political authorities so that it may be in the

position to discountenance with impunity the pathetic cries of those who are most inconveniently affected by her operations. Yet she blows such a loud trumpet about the assistance she renders to peoples in her areas of operations that we cannot but see our neglect as a specially deliberate one.

This act is pellucidly demonstrated in her refusal to control the present catastrophe. About a fortnight ago, there occurred an eruption of crude oil from one oil well. This has developed from one stage to the other until at present the earth is quaking to the discomfort of people both day and night. We see as a calculated attempt to stand by and watch with joy the area sink in the earthquake so that she can more conveniently siphon out the Oil. This is heinously immoral.

The havoc done by the eruption is unprecedented. An area of about four square miles has been perpetually rendered inarable. The farmlands are flooded with crude oil, an old woman was saved the other day from drowning in the crude oil in her farm by some expatriate employees of the Company (it should be noted with all amount of seriousness that the areas so affected are areas newly cultivated by people whose ribs can still be counted as a result of the war). Our rivers, rivulets and creeks are all covered with crude oil. This is unfavourable for breeding of fish; fishing is one of our occupations. We no longer breathe the natural oxygen, rather we inhale lethal and ghastly gases. Our water can no longer be drunk unless one wants to test the effect of crude oil on the body. We no longer use vegetables, they are all polluted. The effect of this explosion casts serious doubts on the minds of people as to whether DERE can survive the imminent famine that will afflict her subsequently. No one can predict with certainty or precision the future of Dere. We are all alarmed. We are all worried. The cup is full. Full to the brim. No, it can no longer take more.

The present unforgettable and unpardonable episode aside, it would be expedient if we look in retrospect into the Shell-BP - Dere (Bomu) relations since 1958. In February of that year when we joined the Company in celebrating the discovery of oil in DERE, we thought we were celebrating prosperity, good health, good education, employment opportunities. But we know now that we were celebrating our entry into a darkened and oblique horizon of despondency, abject poverty, extinction of our lives and destruction of our crops. We thought our town was to be placed on the map of oil producing towns in Nigeria. But to our utmost dismay, our town is *wittingly misnomered BOMU. This is injustice. One is often taken aback to note that a mention of DERE (BOMU) instantaneously disqualifies anyone who wants to seek employment into the Company. This is most unfair.*

Our people are predominantly farmers. The amount of land deprivation suffered by our people is great. The constructions of block station, flow stations, pipelines, waste pits, burrow pits, access roads, etc. have contributed in no mean measure to the terrible reduction of our arable lands.

You are all living witnesses to the amount of disaster our people have suffered as a result of the Company's operations on our land. The fate of 20,000 virile inhabitants of Dere is now in the hands of the Company. Only the Company can supply a solution to our present plight.

We are grieved.

Yours in distress,

MR PANEDOM BADOM
C/O DERE STATE SCHOOL, DERE - OGONI.

CC:
1. *The Managing Director, Shell-BP, Marina - Lagos*
2. *Head of Operations, Eastern Operations, Shell-BP, Box 263, Port-Harcourt.*
3. *Public Relations Officer, Public Relations Dept. Shell-BP, Box 263, Port Harcourt.*
4. *The Secretary to the Military Government, Rivers State, PortHarcourt.*
5. *The Permanent Secretary, Ministry of Agriculture, Fisheries & Natural Resources, Port Harcourt.*
6. *The Permanent Secretary, Federal Ministry of Mines & Power, Lagos.*
7. *The Director of Information, Ministry of Local Govt. & Information, Port Harcourt.*
8. *The Editor, Daily Times, Lagos*
9. *Chiefs and Elders, Dere - Gokana, Ogoni*
10. *The Divisional Officer, Bori - Ogoni, Rivers State*
11. *The Secretary, Eedee Dere.*
12. *Members of Executive Committee, Dere Youths Association.*

DERE STUDENTS' UNION,
DERE GOKANA,
OGONI.
JULY 27, 1970

THE MANAGER,
SHELL-B.P. COMPANY OF NIGERIA LTD.
BOX 263,
PORT HARCOURT.

Sir,

DAMAGES DONE TO OUR LIFE-LINE BY THE CONTINUED PRESENCE OF SHELL-B.P. COMPANY OF NIGERIA. HER INSTALLATIONS AND EXPLORATION OF CRUDE OIL ON OUR SOIL AND ADEQUATE COMPENSATIONS THERE OF.

We the students of Dere - (misnomered BOMU-OIL FIELD by SHELL-B.P.) have been watching with suppressed disgust the considerable amount of damages, sufferings, inconveniences and the economic predicaments borne by us as students in particular and our sponsors, parents, guardians, and guarantors in general, done to our careers, land, sea and creeks and our atmospheric airspace by the oil-exploration of SHELL-B.P. in our AREA of abode.

SHELL-B.P. has since April 1957 that she came to prospect oil in DERE (BOMU) rendered the following grave wave of destruction, pestilence and nuisance to - land, crops and us, as visibly evident to all visitors to the Area:

1. NOISE: There is perpetual high-pitch noise emanating from all SHELL B.P. heavy vibrating machines, trucks and Rig-heads. The deafening effect of the cumulative frequencies of all such noise can besides being alarming, be very serious. We have all turned shouters, hooters, and howlers not speakers.

As students our concentration during holidays are greatly hampered, not to mention the adverse effect profound noise has on the mental, sensory and nervous systems of human beings.

2. **HEAT:** *There is the continuous daily blazing of natural gas rich in all such poisonous, rare and dangerous gases as hydrogen, methane, argon and some cyanide. Tremendous heat is thus radiated.*

(ii) The heat radiated by the blaze is considerable enough to cause uneasiness and discomfort at moments of deep concentration.

(iii) The heat radiated also has terrible bad effects on crops, plants and all living soil-cells. The result of which is infertile land and poor harvest.

(iv) The flame of the gas is not luminous. Thus unburnt carbon is daily being concentrated in the immediate air-space. That's atmospheric pollution.

3. **OIL WELLS:** *(a) Considering that DERE (BOMU) at present possesses to the order of (50) fifty oil-wells worth millions of pounds in WORLD MARKET, we are earnestly speaking of land waste or fertile land being converted barren. All oil-locations are well-spanned by tarred roads and all location premises are cemented. Due to exhaustive reaction of crude oil with soil-cells, immediate farm areas surrounding all such locations become barren and or harvest very poor.*

(b) The conveyance of crude oil under high-pressure in pipe-lines to the magnitude of 6 - 8 lines intertwines or runs the entire length of our farmlands. This is not only waste of arable land but the dangers of burst-pipes and explosions are pertinent. All such explosions and burst-pipes as occurs have tremendous adverse effect on crops, soil and plants due to spouting crude oil.

HORROR: *On Sunday 19th July 1970 a ghastly, grave situation completely out-of-control broke loose.*

Due to gross negligence on the part of SHELL-B.P., pressure over-developed in one of her Well-Heads (CHRISTMAS TREE) and erupted into a Volcano of Crude Oil.

It's running into its second week of an uncontrolled FOUNTAIN of CRUDE OIL flooding farmlands, ravaging crops, polishing fishing-ports; creeks, rivers and riverlets, mangrove forest, suffocating plants.

Streams and the entire air space are dangerously polluted. In earnest, we are all breathing vaporized crude oil in DERE at present and for how long, indefinite. This is horror and disaster at bay.

We have earnestly been too humble, very stupidly co-operative and frankly over-patient.

For considering:

i. That our only pride and well-wishers as students are our parents, guardians, sponsors and guarantors.

ii. That all these categories of our people have just returned rag-tagged from the hell of the Civil War and were just struggling to re-group and reconciliate the lost with the meagre sharable present.

iii. That their only means of resuscitating, maintaining and seeing us through the schools, Colleges and Universities is by their occupation.

iv. That their only occupation is fishing and farming.

v. (a) That farming is done on land - fertile land unpolluted and or flooded by ravishing crude oil.

(b) That fishing is successful only in clear salt or fresh water, creeks, rivers and riverlets and mangrove forest untanned with pestilent crude oil.

vi. That all such occupation entails maintaining a physically strong and healthy body.

vii. That a physically strong and healthy body opts principally for good food to eat, soft fresh air to inhale and clean water to drink.

viii. That all our happiness, satisfaction and contention are fermenting now at home just because of the nuisance of SHELL-B.P.

ix. That we must continue our quest for knowledge and education; then the world stands not to blame us if we as OIL AFFECTED STUDENTS should demand adequate and substantial compensation for all the havoc, horror and nuisance of SHELL-B.P. in DERE.

Our life-line is being strangled, our pride badly and bitterly hurt and our patience can no longer be over-stretched.

We believe that meaningful negotiations can help find solutions to the abject situation. We would not like to be underestimated or taken for a ride by the nose or pushed to place of last resort. The Courts of Justice.

We have the pains, sufferings and difficulties of our guardians, parents, sponsors, guarantors and the entire sixteen thousand poor relations, friends and people of DERE, painfully laden in our heats.

We believe you shall meet with our demands for all such damages and

compensations thereof.
We highly value your uttermost co-operation in this situation.

Thanks.
Yours very sincerely,

(Sgd) NEDOM A. B. D.
SECRETARY, PUBLIC RELATIONS (D. S. U.)
c/o St. Pius X Secondary School,
Bodo, Ogoni.
Rivers State.

(Sgd) C. D. KPAKOL,
PRESIDENT
c/o Government Comprehensive Sec. School,
Port Harcourt, Rivers State.
cc:-

1.   *The Public Relation Officer, Shell-B.P. Port Harcourt.*
2.   *The Manager, Shell-B.P., Port Harcourt.*
3.   *The General Manager, Shell-B.P. Lagos.*
4.   *The Permanent Secretary, Ministry of Mines & Power, Lagos.*
5.   *The Federal Commissioner, Ministry of Mines & Power, Lagos.*
6.   *The Federal Commissioner, Ministry of Education, Lagos*
7.   *The Commissioner for Education, Rivers State, Port-Harcourt*
8.   *The Commissioner for Agriculture and Natural Resources, Rivers State, Port Harcourt.*
9.   *The Divisional Officer, Bori, Ogoni.*
10. *The Dere Town Council, Dere, Gokana, Ogoni.*
11. *The Patron, Dere Students' Union, Dere, Gokana, Ogoni.*
12. *Members of the Executive Committee, Dere Students' Union, Dere, Gokana, Ogoni.*

The reaction of the Federal Government and the media both national and international to the disaster was a deafening silence. No aid was sent to the area. In utter frustration, the Committee of Ogoni Citizens sent the following letter to the London-based weekly newsmagazine, "West Africa":

The Editor,
Overseas Newspapers Ltd.,
Cromwell House,
Fulwood Place,
London, W.C.1.

Dear Sir,

It is amazing that a major disaster such as the blow-out at the Bomu oil-fields got a mere passing note in your esteemed weekly West Africa (August 8, 1970); more so, as your Correspondent was in Port Harcourt during the event.

The blow-out lasted three weeks, devastated extensive areas of farmland, polluted drinking water and air, covered creeks and rivers with a thick layer of oil and sand. Over 20,000 people were deprived of a means of livelihood. Light tremors were felt and children coughed up blood. Up to the time of writing, not an iota of badly needed relief has reached the distressed in the town of Dere. The women marchers are still without drinking water and food. They inhaled methane gas for days.

The incident and the conspiracy of silence that has surrounded it underline quite clearly the plight of the agriculture-minded and minority Ogoni people on whose valuable and limited land (average: 600 per square mile) oil has been found. So long as millions of pounds in royalties accrue to governments and profits to Shell-BP., no one cares for the people who are despoiled in the search for oil.

You might for once oblige your readers with the effect of the discovery of oil on the people on whose land oil is found, rather than the normal worthless and endless computations of how many millions Nigeria is due to get in foreign exchange earnings from petroleum.

Meantime, here is a popular song badly translated from the Ogoni dialect:

> The flames of Shell are hell
> We bask beneath their light
> None for us save the blight
> Of cursed neglect and cursed Shell.

(Sgd) L. L. LOOLO
COMMITTEE OF OGONI CITIZENS, BORI

Needless to say, the newsmagazine did not publish the letter.

For a proper understanding of all the issues raised by the Bomu Oil Disaster, we have to turn to a journalist, Oamen Enaholo, who wrote a comprehensive report in the now-defunct newsmagazine, "African Impact" on 4th February, 1971 as follows:

The Bomu (Dere) oil disaster of July 1970 came as a climax to the sufferings of the Ogoni people. A Dere villager said he would never forget July 20, 1970, the day he and other villagers suddenly discovered that one of Shell-BP's oil wells around the village had blown out and was emitting oil and fire. "The blow-out continued day and night for about two months during which we were forbidden to make fire. Without fire, we could neither cook our meals nor smoke tobacco", he added.

The very existence of the people of Dere was threatened when the well, Bomu II, blew out emitting crude oil, sand, water, gas and fire which engulfed the whole area. It destroyed farmlands within a radius of about three miles and left a thick layer of crude oil on the rivers and creeks from Onne to Bodo, a distance which the people gave as eight miles. Consequently, all marine lives in the area were killed and fish traps destroyed. This unfortunate situation has since left the people with little or no food to eat and no water to drink.

The first reaction of Shell-BP was to express distress at the plight of the people in the area because the blow-out took place at harvest time. Indeed, it was harvest time with a difference because the crops destroyed were the peoples first fruit after the civil war and the seedlings were supplied to them by the Government.

It took the company several weeks to bring the well under control. It was "killed" when a relief well, "Bomu 35" was quickly drilled about half a mile from the blow-out. It is into this relief well that the crude oil from the blow out well is now being pumped. It is reliably learnt that Shell-BP will do everything possible to pump all the pools of crude and the thick layer of oil on the rivers and creeks into the relief well.

Having known what Shell-BP has done to recover part of its lost oil, it follows that one would like to know as well what the company has done to alleviate the sufferings of the people whose food crops, economic trees and farmlands have been destroyed and fishing waters polluted by the blow-out.

Surprisingly, nothing concrete has so far been done in this direction.

Although a committee, comprising representatives of Shell-BP, the Rivers State Government and an independent university man (who has been described as a soil micro-biologist) was said to have been set up to assess the damage done to cash and food crops by the blow-out, nothing has so far been heard from the committee. Even if the committee eventually submits its report to the Rivers State Government, it is doubtful whether Ogoni people will accept it.

This is because in a press release by the Committee of Ogoni Citizens on August 15, 1970, it was pointed out that the Ogoni people did not regard as complete or meaningful a body of assessors which did not include direct representatives of the people. The Ogoni citizens also attacked the terms of reference of the assessment committee on the ground that damage was not done to food and cash crops alone as Shell-BP wanted to establish as a prenegotiation posture. "Greater damage was done also to land and soil, drinking water, fishing ground and villages and air", the people added.

Because of the unwillingness of its members to talk it is not yet known how soon the assessment committee will complete its work. A source close to it, however, disclosed that its work has been slowed down to some extent by the long time required to carry out laboratory tests on soil samples taken from the disaster area. Soon after the flow of lava from the blow-out well was completely brought under control, Shell-BP flew some agronomists from overseas to Nigeria to test the soil within the three-mile radius of the blow-out well. The aim was to determine the long term effect of the blow-out on the land. It is also understood that the assessment committee has, for the same reason, carried out some tests on soil samples from the area. The tests were undertaken by the University soil expert member of the committee.

What is in fact reported to be holding back the work of the committee is that its members have not been able to agree on how much should be paid as compensation. A source disclosed that the amount demanded by the Ogoni people has been rejected by Shell-BP representatives on the committee on the ground that it is arbitrary and fantastic.

Scientific Calculation

It is understood that while the company is very anxious to pay compensation without much delay, it insists that whatever it pays must be *based on some scientific calculations. As far as Shell-BP is concerned, it is impossible to assess the long term equitable compensation to the owners of land and farms in the affected area without resorting to some scientific tests and calculations. The people of Ogoni however regard this as a tactic by the company to avoid paying compensations.*

One thing probably responsible for this disagreement is that there is misunderstanding over what constitutes the long term damage to the land and the rivers and creeks. It is believed in some quarters that Shell-BP is planning, as part of its compensation for the long term damage to the farmland, to rehabilitate the affected area so that it will be good enough for cultivation once more. This means that the company will acquire the area for a period of some years during which it will till the land and add all sorts of manures to it until it is fit again for cultivation. As soon as this aim is achieved the land may be handed back to the owners. Shell-BP will of course pay adequate compensations for the land during the period of rehabilitation.

With regard to the damage done to rivers and creeks, it is believed by some observers that it would be necessary for Shell-BP to remove the present blanket of oil from the surface of the water. The revival of marine life in this area would not be possible until the crude oil is removed from the water.

*Whatever happens, there seems to be no justification for delaying the committee's report for such a long time. If members of the committee are in difficulty, it will not be out of place if they borrow a leaf from what happened in the case of previous accidents of this nature. There is the **Tory Canvon** disaster in 1966 off the coast of England. For it, the British Government billed the oil companies and ship owners £3 million (three million pounds) as compensation. Similar claims have recently been made in the case of a Liberian tanker, **Pacific Glory**, which collided with another ship on October 23, 1970, eight miles off St. Catherine's Point, Isle of Wight.*

Although soil scientists and agronomists are attached to the Bomu oil disaster assessment committee, their role is only to determine the extent of damage done to the soil and probably the crops thereon. The question of computation and quantification of the compensation payable is the responsibility of a valuer and this is the practice the world over. The result of soil tests therefore only constitutes a part of data for a valuation exercise, and this exercise would necessarily cover damage to the soil and crops, injurious effect in general, and disturbance to rights and users. One is therefore constrained to ask why the conventionally accepted procedures which are presumed also to be known to the Shell-BP have not been adopted in the Bomu II blow-out.

Because of the grievous harm done to social life in Ogoni and the effect of the blow-out on the physical and mental health of the people, their patience is running out rapidly especially as they have received no relief from anywhere. At a meeting held on September 12, 1970, Ogoni Chiefs, farmers and fishermen expressed grave concern over the increased cost of living in the division and the general scarcity of food and fish following the devastation of the area by the blow-out. They regretted that "hardly any relief has been sent into this disaster area" and therefore appealed to the Rivers State Government and its agencies as well as other humanitarian organizations in the State and elsewhere in the country to send help immediately.

Relief Material

Frankly, it is astonishing that no organization in Nigeria took the Bomu (Dere) oil disaster so seriously as to send relief materials to the people. One would have expected the Nigerian Red Cross Society and other humanitarian organizations in the country to find out the extent of the disaster soon after it occurred and rush in some foodstuff to the area to alleviate the sufferings of the unfortunate victims.

The Committee of Ogoni Citizens felt that Shell-BP Company was, to some extent, responsible for the absence of relief help from organizations and individuals by making the matter look small. In a release issued in August, the committee deplored the attempt by Shell-BP to obscure the seriousness of the social problems created by the blow-out and accused the company of publishing empty promises with an intent to lull the nation into an erroneous belief that there was no cause for alarm.

Looked at from this angle, it would appear that Shell-BP is actually taking advantage of the pitfalls in the Nigeria Law governing the exploration and production of oil. The law stipulates that where oil and agricultural interests clash, agriculture must give way to oil.

The first commercial oil was discovered at Oloibiri in the Rivers State in January 1956 by the Shell-BP Petroleum Development Company. Towards the end of that year, the company made a second discovery at Afam in the East Central State. Intensification of the search for oil led in 1958-59 to the discovery of oil in Ebubu and Bomu in Ogoni division of the Rivers State and at Ughelli in the Midwestern State.

With these discoveries, Shell-BP's production stood at over 6,000 barrels per day in 1958. Today the company's production has increased to about one million barrels a day, while all the oil companies in Nigeria together produce about 1 1/2 (one and half) million barrels per day. It is estimated that overall production of all oil companies will reach two million barrels a day by 1972-73. Up to 1969, oil provided under 20 per cent of the Federal Government's total revenue, but by 1972-73 it may be well over half the total revenue.

Anyone who visits Ogoni division is likely to be surprised by the way the limited farmlands have been turned into oil fields, dotted all over with oil wells, pipelines, flow stations, access-roads and gas flares. One of the farmers in the area said with utter disgust: "I do not know what we have done to make God punish us by bringing Shell-BP into our land. Every year, we spend our time, money and energy to cultivate the land and then, suddenly one day, Shell-BP caterpillars come in to destroy our crops. Any house that falls within the company's area of interest must also be destroyed. Even though we are never adequately compensated, we have nobody to complain to simply because our law stipulates that oil must take precedence over anything else."

The largest concentration of oil wells in Nigeria is in Ogoni division in the Rivers State. In and around Dere (which Shell-BP usually refer to as Bomu) village alone, there are over 40 oil wells and the Ebubu oil field is very large too. Yet, the search for oil continues in every nook and corner of this division.

It is interesting however to note that while many Nigerians regard the discovery of oil in the country as a blessing the people of Ogoni division in general and the people of Dere village in particular have been forced by circumstances to think otherwise. To them, the presence of oil in their area is a curse. In a recent open letter from the Ogoni Students Union, University of Ibadan Branch, to the Shell-BP Petroleum Development Company of

Nigeria Limited, the students stated that "the greatest curse that ever happened to the Ogoni people (especially the people of Gokana and those other places where oil fields are located) is the presence of oil in their God given land". And in an earlier letter to the company, the Dere Students' Union said they had watched with suppressed disgust the sufferings, inconveniences and economic predicaments borne by their people as a result of the presence of oil in their place and the considerable damage done to their land, rivers, creeks and the atmospheric air-space by Shell-BP oil exploration operations in the area.

Grievances

The students are not alone in their grievances against Shell-BP. Their parents and guardians are even more vocal on the matter. When, for example the Rivers State Military Governor, Lt. Commander Diete-Spiff visited the area on August 1, 1970, the people of Dere, in an address of welcome they presented to the Governor, accused Shell-BP of pursuing a "Godless economic policy" in their locality and of profiteering at the expense of their lives by extracting the "liquid god" (oil) from their soil without caring for the welfare of the people in the area.

Anybody who has been to Ogoni recently cannot help sympathizing with the people. Their main occupations are farming and fishing. Yet scarcity of land had been a great problem in the division. At Gokana for example, land pressure was so much that farmers had to cultivate the same piece of land yearly instead of every two or three years. The result was that the yield diminished from year to year. According to a report of the Niger Delta Development Board in 1966, land available in this area of Ogoni division was .08 acre per person per year. That means that about 17 people must share an acre of land for farming. Consequently, the people could not produce even enough food to feed themselves.

The situation has however been worsened by the presence of oil in this area. Shell-BP has acquired the greater part of the land for oil production and has thus left the people with very little land to farm on. Consequently land has become very expensive in this area. As the people said, an acre of land in Gokana costs over £250 (two hundred and fifty pounds).

In spite of this, Shell-BP was paying only £1:10/- per year for an acre of land in this same area. But only recently, the amount payable a year by the company was said to have been increased to £4 (four pounds) per acre. The people complained that the amount payable for farm crops is equally very poor. According to them the company pays only one shilling (1/-) per yam stand and pays very little or nothing at all for other crops like okro, pepper, sugar-cane, tomatoes and beans. These figures are said to be arbitrary, and there is no provision for appeal.

Ten Years of Daylight

This, no doubt, is a disruption of normal life in the village. The people have been used to having 12 hours of day and 12 hours of night. But now, their position is worse than that of the Eskimos in the North Pole for while nature gives the Eskimos six months of daylight followed by six months of night, Shell-BP has given the Dere people about ten years of continuous daylight. There are no compensations for these inconveniences and there is nothing to show that Shell-BP shield the flame from the people.

The worst effect of the blow-out on the lives of the people of Ogoni is that they have already started to move away from oil fields into other areas for fear that another blow-out can happen again at any time. They even dread living or farming close to pipelines. In a recent letter to Shell-BP, Dere students stated that the conveyance of crude oil under high pressure in pipelines all over the farmland constituted an imminent danger of "burst-pipes and explosions".

Looked at closely, it will be foolhardy to regard the people's fears as groundless. The Bomu blow-out has been regarded in several quarters as an accident which is usually common in oil fields. Viewed from this angle, the possibility of similar accidents in the area cannot be ruled out.

These are only some of the sufferings of the people who happen to live around oil fields in Nigeria. Yet, in this country as elsewhere in the world, oil is politics. The significant point here is that the people in whose land oil is found derive no special benefits from the oil other than compensations for food and cash crops, buildings, sacred places and shrines destroyed as a result of oil operations. Normally, compensation for private properties is a direct negotiation between the oil companies and the owners of the properties. The government intervenes only when there is disagreement between the two parties.

All other payments, such as concession rentals, royalties, profits tax and *customs duties are made to the Federal Government. At present there is a complex system by which rents and royalties are divided among the oil producing states and the distributable pool account. Following agitations by the non-oil-producing states the system was slightly amended last March in favour of the pool. That, in theory, means that the non-oil-producing states now get more from oil revenue than they were getting before. They are however not content with what they have already got. They are still claiming that the "oil belongs to all of us" and no state should therefore be given preferential treatment in the sharing of oil revenue. Unlike cocoa, rubber and groundnut which have to be planted, cared for and harvested before yielding revenue, the non-oil-producing states said, oil is a natural resource and the people living in and around oil fields contribute nothing to its production.*

This argument appears to be rather irrelevant because while it is true that oil is a natural resource, it is equally true that nature makes cocoa, rubber and groundnut grow in only certain parts of the federation. That cocoa does not do well in Sokoto is the work of nature over which the Sokoto farmers have no control.

Nigeria's Military leaders have however promised to solve once and for all the burning issue of "re-allocation of revenue" before they hand over to the civilians about 1976. Right now, therefore, one can only hope that the plight of the people living in the oil areas of the country will be taken into account when the time comes to review the nation's revenue allocation policy.

It is however not enough to sit in Lagos or elsewhere and abstractly produce a formula for the allocation of revenue derived from oil. It is necessary for all practical purposes for those charged with this responsibility to visit the oil producing areas so that they may be better enabled to appreciate the misery, risks to life and property, and all the other inconveniences affecting the people under whose land oil is produced for the purposes of revenue allocation. It may not be too much to ask that a proportion of the royalties, no matter how small, be paid directly to the local authority in whose area oil is produced, for the provision of basic amenities and the alleviation of some of the sufferings of these people.

Oamen Enaholo's article contains one inaccuracy. It is true that a

Committee was set up by the Rivers State Government to assess the damage done by the blow-out and establish what compensation should be paid by Shell-B.P. However, no representative of Shell-B.P. sat on the Committee.

The Committee, of which I was a member, worked extremely hard and produced a report. The Official Secrets Act forbids my releasing that report at this time, but I can confirm that it was established that Shell-B.P.'s negligence in installing outdated equipment led to considerable harm being done and that compensation running into tens of millions of pounds was due to be paid by Shell-B.P. to the people of Dere and the surrounding area.

The Committee also made far-reaching and long-term proposals for rehabilitation and resettlement of the area which would have cost tens of millions of pounds.

What the Committee had not counted on was the deviousness of Shell-B.P. and the lack of interest of the Federal Government of Nigeria in the affair. Just as the Committee was about to submit its report to the Rivers State Executive Council, news came that a section of the Dere Community had sued Shell-B.P. to court claiming a compensation of £250,000 (two hundred and fifty thousand pounds).

And in totally uncharacteristic fashion, the High Court of Rivers State delivered judgement in the shortest possible time, entering judgement in the sum of £168,468.5.9d (one hundred and sixty-eight thousand four hundred and sixty-eight pounds, five shillings and nine pence) which Shell had admitted. Once again, Shell had cheated the poor peasants. The British-born judge who joined in this rape of the Ogoni people was soon to be knighted by the Queen of England. While I cannot state categorically that the honour was won as a result of the judgement in respect of the Bomu Oil Disaster, I must say that I harbour that suspicion. Efforts by the Rivers State Government to interest the Federal Military Government in the matter yielded no fruit whatsoever. General Yakubu Gowon, who was Head of State at the time, visited the wasteland created by the blow-out during a visit to Rivers State in 1971. He stood before it incomprehensibly, staring tongue-tied, unable to say even a word of comfort to the affected villagers or to order that even the minutest relief be sent to the area. His famed Christian conscience was not even touched.

Today, twenty-two years after, the wasteland remains - barren and useless, another reminder of the road to the extinction of the Ogoni people charted by the greed and racism of Shell and the complicity of the Federal Government of Nigeria.

Since then, the offending oil well has been capped, new wells dug, and gas from them has been burning methane and other hydrocarbons into the lungs of Ogoni villagers every day of the year for twenty-one years. The noise of burning gas has made the people of Dere half-deaf - they have to shout when they speak to each other; burning gas continues to turn their nights into day. They have no electricity, no pipe-borne water and no hospital. Respiratory diseases are common in the area. Only last year, the entire village was flooded because the access roads built by Shell to its numerous locations have made a valley of the village. Studies have indicated that the level of lead in the blood of the inhabitants is at a dangerously high level.

Shell must bear full responsibility for the genocide of the Ogoni which is going on even now. The record of the Company in environmental issues in Nigeria has been most appalling. When Chevron began to prospect for oil in Ogoni twelve years ago in 1980, it had the example of Shell to go by.

The most notorious action of both companies has been the flaring of gas, sometimes in the middle of villages, as in Dere, (Bomu Oilfield) or very close to human habitation as in the Yorla and Korokoro oilfields in Ogoni. This action has destroyed ALL wildlife, and plant life, poisoned the atmosphere and therefore the inhabitants in the surrounding areas and made the residents half-deaf and prone to respiratory diseases. Whenever it rains in Ogoni, all we have is acid rain which further poisons water courses, streams, creeks and agricultural land.

Next to the flaring of gas comes the frequency of oil spills. Shell and Chevron use the most outdated equipment and technology in Ogoni, leading to innumerable oil spills which destroy farmlands, streams and water courses and the creeks. One of the greatest casualties of oil spills has been the mangrove trees in the swamps which near-surround Ogoni. These trees which were a source of firewood, of seafood such as oysters, mussels, crabs and cockles, have been unable to survive the toxicity of oil. They have now been replaced by strange, valueless palms.

Additionally, oil has poisoned the mudbanks which were formerly the home of mudskippers, clams, crabs and periwinkles. These rich sources of protein for the Ogoni people no longer exist. The result is that the fishermen of Ogoni have lost their occupation and Ogoni people no longer have protein in their food. Children are the main sufferers at the hands of Shell and Chevron.

Similarly, the pollution of water courses, streams and creeks by oil spillage has led to the death of another source of protein - fish. As indicated in Chapter 1, these streams and creeks formerly brimmed with fish. Today, the Ogoni who normally fished in these waters have no alternatives. If they must fish, they need to go into deeper and offshore waters for which they have not been equipped or trained.

Pipelines criss-cross Ogoni territory, using up valuable land and ringing the people round with the danger of oil being pumped under very high pressure. These pipes metaphorically drain the very life-blood of the Ogoni people. As the oil mining activities of Shell and Chevron proceed apace, huge company trucks and other vehicle thunder past villages and towns day and night, an additional hazard to the peace and quiet of rural life.

As a final mark of their genocidal intent and insensitivity to human suffering, Shell and Chevron refuse to obey a Nigerian law which requires all oil companies to re-inject gas into the earth rather than flare it. Shell and Chevron think it cheaper to poison the atmosphere and the Ogoni and pay the paltry penalty imposed by the government of Nigeria than re-inject the gas as stipulated by the regulations.

To this charge of genocidal intent and insensitivity to human suffering must be added another of racism. Shell has won prizes for environmental protection in Europe where it also prospects for oil. So it cannot be that it does not know what to do. Now, why has it visited the Ogoni people with such horror as I have merely outlined here? The answer must lie in racism. In Shell's racist mind, what is good for the whites must not be good for blacks.

Shell has used its financial might to promote European culture in Nigeria. It regularly sponsors the tours of British artists to Nigeria, but spends nothing on the promotion of Ogoni culture. It is, at this moment, sponsoring the construction of a theatre for chamber music in Lagos at a cost of twenty million naira (one million pounds). But it has not spent a tenth of that amount in Ogoni in thirty-four years of exploitation of Ogoni resources estimated at a total value of 100 billion US dollars.

Added to this charge is that of ethnocentrism which Shell has promoted in Nigeria. Shell's best residential and office blocks in Nigeria are situated in Lagos among the Yoruba ethnic majority where there is not a drop of crude oil. It does not have a single modern building in Ogoni. Chevron pays more in rent in one year for ONE two-bedroom flat for one of its middle-level employees in Lagos among the Yorubas than it has paid in a total of ten years to the Ogoni landlords whose land it is expropriating. Both Shell and Chevron ensure that their best jobs and contracts go first to foreigners and then to the ethnic majority in Nigeria.

Shell has stated that its sole responsibility is to produce hydrocarbons efficiently. This is manifestly false. Shell and other companies routinely contribute to the social and economic well-being of the people among whom they operate. Indeed, it is a datum of management wisdom to create a conducive atmosphere for business operations. Why Shell and Chevron have decided pig-headedly to oppress, suppress and eventually destroy the Ogoni people cannot be understood. How they can take away millions of dollars from a people who have no electricity, no pipe-borne water, no hospitals, no schools and no future and feel no pangs of conscience whatsoever defies the imagination.

The result of the foregoing has been the total destruction of Ogoni life, human, social, cultural and economic. I have already outlined in Chapter 1 the intrinsic psychic relationship which exists between the Ogoni and their environment. What Shell and Chevron have done to Ogoni people, land, streams, creeks and the atmosphere amount to genocide. The soul of the Ogoni people is dying and I am witness to the fact.

I hear the plaintive cry of the Ogoni plains mourning the birds that no longer sing at dawn; I hear the dirge for trees whose branches wither in the blaze of gas flares, whose roots lie in infertile graves. The brimming streams gurgle no more, their harvest floats on waters poisoned by oil spillages.

Where are the antelopes, the squirrels, the sacred tortoises, the snails, the lions and tigers which roamed this land? Where are the crabs, periwinkles, mudskippers, cockles, shrimps and all which found sanctuary in mudbanks, under the protective roots of mangrove trees?

I hear in my heart the howls of death in the polluted air of my beloved home-land; I sing a dirge for my children, my compatriots and their progeny.

CHAPTER 6

THE NAIL IN THE OGONI COFFIN

I have indicated how the oil of the Ogoni and other minorities in the delta provided part of the hidden agenda of the Nigerian Civil War (1967-70). I have also shown the intense suffering of the Ogoni people as a result of the battle for the control of the oilfields.

The war soon did end in victory for the Federal forces. But even before the war ended, the Federal Government had begun to plot against the Ogoni and other minorities. A Commission (the Dina Commission) was set up to explore ways of expropriating the rights of the inhabitants of the oil-bearing areas.

The Independence Constitution of 1960 and the Republican Constitution of 1963 spelt out clearly the principles for sharing revenue derived from each part of the Federation:

"There shall be paid by the Federation to each Region a sum equal to fifty per cent of (a) the proceeds of any royalty received by the Federation in respect of any minerals in that Region; and (b) any mining rents derived by the Federation from within that Region."

The Dina Commission headed by a member of the Yoruba ethnic majority, recommended that the States of origin be now paid only FIVE per cent of such royalties and mining rents. A meeting of State officials (which I attended, representing Rivers State) rejected the recommendation.

General Gowon, the then military ruler of Nigeria ignored this rejection and went on to decree the complete confiscation by the Federal Government of all off-shore oil in defiance of the Constitution negotiated by all Nigerians. This action was to usher in that armed robbery of the Ogoni and other delta minorities which has been the hallmark of Nigerian life from 1970 until this moment.

Because of the multi-ethnic nature of Nigerian society, most Nigerians pay only lip service to the concept of a Nigerian nation state, and what is "Nigerian" property is mostly regarded as belonging to no one. Also, most Nigerians, including their rulers, owe their first loyalty to their ethnic groups. General Gowon's illegal seizure of offshore oil enriched the Federal treasury. And the lootocrats based in Lagos proceeded to misappropriate these funds, sending most of it to their ethnic areas.

By 1972, oil had become not only a huge revenue earner but also the central focus of all the murderous political plots, double dealing, chicanery, lying, cheating and corruption of the ethnic majority of Nigeria.

From 1956 there had been a clamour for the creation of States to lessen ethnic tension and afford the minorities an opportunity to achieve self-determination and so create a more just and democratic society. The 12-state structure established in 1967 before the civil war was a step in this direction but there were still demands for states on the part of the dispossessed minorities.

In 1975, General Gowon was overthrown in a coup by his lieutenants. The new men immediately headed for the oil resources of the Ogoni and other delta minorities. They created seven new states, most of them in the ethnic majority areas of the Hausa-Fulani, Igbo and Yoruba, increasing thereby the share of oil revenues by these groups while exacerbating ethnic tension. They went further to revise the revenue allocation formula agreed before independence, so to give the ethnic majorities a still greater share of oil revenue. The areas from which oil was being extracted were now forced to accept twenty per cent instead of fifty per cent of the proceeds of mining rents and royalties.

In 1979, the military dictatorship further usurped the fundamental economic rights of the Ogoni and other oil producing minorities securing dubious respectability for this usurpation by having it inscribed in the 1979 Constitution, Section 42 (3) of which states: *Notwithstanding the foregoing provisions of this section, the entire property in and control of all minerals, mineral oils and natural gas in, under or upon any land in Nigeria or in, under or upon the territorial waters and the Exclusive Economic Zone of Nigeria shall vest in the Government of the Federation, and shall be managed in such manner as may be prescribed by the National Assembly.*

This expropriation of the fundamental economic right of the ethnic groups which make up the Nigerian federation is peculiar to Nigeria. Only the Soviet Union under the Communists ever tried it. But then the Soviets assumed full responsibility for the education, housing, and medical needs of all citizens. The ethnic majority in Nigeria which passed this ridiculous law under the supervision of the military had no such lofty aim. They had succeeded in institutionalizing theft.

But the dictatorial military were not done. They proceeded to smuggle a "Land Use Decree" into the Constitution. Under the decree, all land in Nigeria was said to be owned by the Federal Government! The military had not bothered to have the Constituent Assembly debate this all-important provision. They simply wrote it into the Constitution. And that was that.

The Head of State and Commander-in-Chief of the Armed Forces at the time was General Olusegun Obasanjo, a Yoruba. He soon handed over power to Shehu Shagari, of the Hausa-Fulani who got Dr Pius Okigbo, a brilliant Igbo economist to devise a revenue allocation formula for the consideration of the National Assembly. By the time Dr Okigbo was done, the oil producing minorities had been apportioned but two per cent of their property. Dr G. B. Leton, an Ogoni, who sat on the Revenue Allocation Commission, predictably submitted a dissenting view in a Minority Report which was as predictably thrown out.

The refusal of the ethnic majority to pay mining rents and royalties to the Ogoni and other delta minorities confirms their genocidal intentions. It should be noted that the main revenue from oil to the Federal Government lies in Petroleum Profits Tax which the Government continues to collect and keep. So that there can be no honest reason for failing to keep to agreements reached by the federating ethnic units before independence.

Thieves normally operate by night, or if they must move in daytime, they often wear a mask. The ethnic majority in Nigeria are too cowardly to steal by night and dare not wear a mask. They prefer bare-faced, daylight robbery. Their victims? The Ogoni and such delta minorities.

The daylight robbers proclaim their skulduggery loud, thumping their chest in self-congratulation. Mr Philip Asiodu, one-time Permanent Secretary in the Federal Ministry of Mines and Power and currently a Director of Chevron and a regular in the corridors of power to this day, said in a public lecture in 1980:

> Like (sic) in many other areas of the world, the regions
> where oil is found in this country are very inhospitable.
> They are mainly in swamps and creeks. They require
> massive injection of money if their conditions and
> standards of living are to compare with what obtains

*elsewhere in the country where possibilities of agriculture
and diversified industry are much greater. There is a
nudging acceptance of the special needs of oil areas in the
latest proposals being discussed by the government but I
believe there is a long way to go to meet the claims of the
oil producing areas which see themselves losing non-
replaceable resources while replaceable and permanent
resources of agriculture and industry are being developed
elsewhere largely with oil revenue. Given, however, the
small size and population of the oil-producing areas, it is
not cynical to observe that even if the resentments of oil
producing states continue, they cannot threaten the stability
of the country nor affect its continued economic
development.*

The language of colonialism. Even the Europeans did not treat the
colonized with such open contempt. But what will you have? Mr P. C.
Asiodu is President of the World Wildlife Fund in Nigeria and has drunk tea
with the Duke of Edinburgh. I have the impression that he would like the
Ogoni and other people in the oil-bearing areas to turn to beasts of burden
so that his cynicism and his presidency of the Wildlife Fund might bear
fruit.

That nearly came to pass by January 1984 when President Shehu Shagari
was overthrown. In spite of a ballooning treasury enriched by oil which sold
at forty dollars per barrel at some point, Shagari managed to spend all the
money - on nothing - and then to go steeply into debt to Western banks and
institutions, effectively turning Nigerians born and unborn into debt peonage.
Most of the money borrowed was used for projects in the ethnic majority
areas -in the birthplaces of the wielders of power. Whatever benefits were
incurred went to these areas. And where the money ended up in private
pockets, as it often did, it was the pocket of a member of the ethnic majority
as was shown in the corruption inquiries which followed Shagari's
overthrow.

Meanwhile, the two per cent of oil revenue which was meant to be paid
to those in the oil-bearing areas, remained unpaid for all sorts of
unacceptable reasons.

After the overthrow of Shagari, the military under General Muhammadu Buhari (another Hausa-Fulani oppressor) meanly reduced the revenue to be paid to oil-producing states to one and a half per cent, which it still refused to pay, choosing to lend the money which had accumulated over the years to bankrupt states mostly in the ethnic majority areas.

This is all very tiresome, but historical accuracy demands that it all be properly documented.

What finally sealed the fate of the Ogoni was the seizure of power by General Ibrahim Babangida whose regime openly promoted the interest of the Hausa-Fulani and Yoruba and to some extent, the Igbos. The worst of its actions was the creation in 1991 of eleven new states and the increase of local governments to almost six hundred. None of the States or local governments so created except those in the oil-bearing areas is viable. Quite apart from the fact that political structures should not be set up as a means of sharing revenue, the entire exercise was terribly unjust and immoral.

For instance, the Yoruba, Hausa and Igbo live in contiguous areas and should therefore be administered each in a single State. By the Babangida wisdom, the Hausa, Yoruba and Igbo are today administered in 10, 6 and 5 States each. None of these States can pay their way. They all live, vampire-like, on the resources of the Ogoni and the delta minorities whose land has oil.

Similarly, the local governments were set up by no discernible criteria, and resulted in varying sizes and configurations. They all depended on subventions provided by oil money. In allocating the subventions, the administration regarded them, strangely, as equal and sent them almost equal sums of money. Since each local government is expected to bear responsibility for primary education, those areas with 50,000 pupils as in Ogoni find that they cannot pay teachers and children have been out of school for almost one year. Yet other local government areas have but 2,000 pupils, pay teachers regularly and have surplus funds.

Allocation of revenue to the states also followed criteria which were clearly dishonest. Such parameters as equality of states, land mass (but excluding the revenue-providing seas), population and internally-generated revenue were used whenever they proved handy to those in power. What was equal about the states? Nothing. And who knew the true population of each state? No one. Everything was being done to transfer the oil resources of the Ogoni and other delta minorities to the non-oil producing areas of the country.

The result is that whereas the Ogoni are out of school, in Borno State in the arid north, there is free education at primary, secondary and tertiary levels!

Analyzing why Nigeria's First Republic was "a disastrous and unmitigated failure", Obafemi Awolowo listed, among others, "the allocation of revenue" which, according to him, "was done in such a manner as to outrage the feelings of those sections of Nigeria which are at the main source of derivation and to induce a sense of financial irresponsibility in some of the other sections." (*Path to Nigerian Greatness* p. 32).

Awolowo also indicates that in the creation of states, politicians in power have been "unashamedly illogical, spiteful, unprincipled and opportunistic." This was as true in the 1960s as in the seventies, eighties and nineties.

Under the military dictatorships which have ruled the country from 1967 to this year (1992), the determination has been to subvert the federal culture of the country, establish a unitary state, corner the oil resources of the nation at the centre and then have these resources transferred by the Big Man who has come to power either by electoral fraud or military coup to the ethnic majority areas.

Forcing the Ogoni to remain in a multi-ethnic State such as Rivers State is to further marginalize them. Twenty-five years of running Rivers State has shown that such multi-ethnic states are not workable, UNLESS the ethnic groups have a Constitution which binds them along lines agreed BEFORE the establishment of the State.

In Rivers State, the majority Ijaws are more interested in their own welfare than in establishing a fair and just state. The constituent ethnic groups spend more time fighting for the crumbs which fall from Nigeria's Federal table at which the ethnic majorities preside, than in creating social and economic progress. In short, Rivers State is but a microcosm of Nigeria in which the majority ethnic groups triumph while the minorities gnash their teeth in agony. But it is even worse because the multi-ethnic Rivers State is run as a unitary state without the nod which is made at the centre towards federalism. In such a situation, such ethnic minorities as the Ogoni are condemned to slavery and extinction.

Thus, political structuring and revenue allocation have been used to completely marginalize the Ogoni, grossly abusing their rights and veritably consigning them to extinction.

Beyond political structuring and revenue allocation, the very administration of the Nigerian nation has worked against the Ogoni because the wielders of power - the ethnic majorities - operate by cheating. Appointments to plum jobs in the military, the civil service and the parastatals are not based on merit but on jobbery, favouritism and chicanery. Jobs are not advertised; they go to tribesmen, family members and friends, whether they have the qualification or not.

In the 1970s in the wake of the oil boom, the Federal Government decided that it would control "the commanding heights of the economy" and went on to involve itself in every possible business venture. Twenty years later all such business had virtually collapsed and were existing on government subvention, (for which read oil money) their only beneficiaries being their managers who are almost always from the majority ethnic groups.

Nothing works in Nigeria because rulers and ruled owe loyalty, not to the country, but to their ethnic groups. Theft of government funds is not considered a crime because the nation lives on oil money which rightly belongs, not to everyone or to the government, but to the ethnic minorities who are in no position to control it.

The National Bank of Nigeria was established in 1933 by the Yorubas and it was a modest success when the cocoa boom aided Yoruba farmers and traders to unprecedented heights of prosperity in the 50s and 60s. By 1992, it filed for bankruptcy, having been brought to its knees by its mainly Yoruba directors and clients. Unsecured loans were of the order of 1 billion naira. Indeed, the entire banking system in Nigeria is known to be a massive fraud which benefits the wielders of power exclusively.

In similar fashion, the University system is also a fraud. Every state that is created sets up what it purports to be a University. But only the ethnic majority in Nigeria believes that a University can exist without books and equipment. Yet, degrees get regularly awarded.

The availability of seized oil money also encourages the ethnic majority to indulge in dubious expensive ventures. One of these is the attempt of the Federal Government to magic wheat out of the sands of the savannah. The delta home of the ethnic minorities which belches forth petrodollars also can produce swamp rice to feed the whole of West Africa. Rather than encourage the growth of rice in natural conditions, the government is throwing money recklessly after wheat - just to benefit the ethnic majority.

In the administration of justice which is the bastion of truth, the ethnic factor also plays a role. Judges are likely to wink at crime depending on the ethnic origin of the criminal.

Thus, the nation state is quite irrelevant to the Nigerian. What matters is the ethnic group. Dr Ishrat Husain, former World Bank representative in Nigeria reporting his experience in the country, said: "The paradox of Nigeria baffled me. No other country with this country's depth of human and material resources can let itself into all the problems in Nigeria today."

The paradox inheres in the political and administrative structuring of the country. As organized today, the country is not a workable possibility. There is no country. There is only organized brigandage. The pity of it is that it should have had the blessing of the international community which allows it its investment, technology and credit, all of which have been completely wasted. Under the present political and administrative structure of Nigeria, the country will never be able to pay the debts it owes the international banks. Why is the international community supporting the massive fraud that is the Nigerian nation?

David and Audrey Smock in their book, *The Politics of Pluralism* assert:
> *Events in the last decade attest to the fact that communal attachments do not quietly wither away with the exposure to modernizing influences. Quite the contrary, modernization often creates the very conditions necessary for the incubation of strong communal identities and sets the stage for communal competition.*

Nigeria proves it. Such communal competition breeds dictatorship which then strangles the weak and powerless, and all ideas of democracy.

The genocide of the Ogoni bears witness to the fact.

CHAPTER 7

THE AUTONOMY OPTION

In 1990, the Ogoni people took stock of their situation in Nigeria and found that for all the wealth of their land, and in spite of the fact that an estimated 100 billion US dollars had been taken from the land in thirty two years of oil mining, they had no schools, no hospitals and no roads. They found that there was intense pressure on their land and that they lived in a poisoned environment in which wildlife, etc. could not survive. They found that the few Ogoni men and women who had some education, had no access whatsoever to jobs and that when they had jobs at all, they did not obtain promotion, no matter their competence. They found that from time, their leaders had laid faith in co-operation with the rest of Nigeria but that this faith had been grievously misplaced as each ethnic group had its own agenda quite unrelated to the notion of co-operation in a multi-ethnic nation.

They found that, in plain terms, they were being terribly exploited in the name of a Nigeria to which no one paid fealty or only nominal fealty and only in so for as it enabled them to advance their personal or ethnic interests. They found that the tribulations which they had suffered in the civil war and ever since would not end unless they took their fate into their own hands. They also found that they had lost a sense of community; that their best men were in exile in different parts of the country and that this was contrary to the order among other ethnic groups where men and women could achieve success in ten or twenty different centres WITHIN their ethnic home areas. They found that their languages were dying and they still lived in mudhuts and dilapidated villages unfit for beasts.

They also found that the Nigeria of which they were a part was deeply in debt in spite of the enormous resources which they had contributed to it; that it was getting deeper into debt and that the only way those debts could ever be repaid was by the exploitation of Ogoni resources, which exploitation would do even more harm to Ogoni existence.

And they knew that the only thing that could make the eighth oil-producing country in the world also the thirteenth poorest was gross mismanagement by the ethnic majority who wielded power in the country.

And it became obvious to them that the country was headed in a wrong direction and that something would have to be done urgently to alter their situation and the situation of the country, if all was not to be lost.

That thing was none other than the operation of either a true federation in which each ethnic group would have autonomy and be directly responsible for its own salvation, a confederation of equal States based on its ethnic groups or the complete disintegration of the country with each ethnic group left to fend for itself. They voted for the first option. And they decided to put the nation to the test.

Accordingly, their Chiefs and leaders decided to test the waters. They addressed an Ogoni Bill of Rights to the Nigerian President, General Babangida and his Armed Forces Ruling Council who had seized power in 1985 and had been running the nation according to their whims and caprices ever since:

OGONI BILL OF RIGHTS

PRESENTED TO THE GOVERNMENT AND PEOPLE OF NIGERIA

We, the people of Ogoni (Babbe, Gokana, Ken Khana, Nyo Khana and Tai) numbering about 500,000 being a separate and distinct ethnic nationality within the Federal Republic of Nigeria, wish to draw the attention of the Governments and people of Nigeria to the undermentioned facts:

1. That the Ogoni people, before the advent of British colonialism, were not conquered or colonized by any other ethnic group in present-day Nigeria.
2. That British colonization forced us into the administrative division of Opobo from 1908 to 1947.
3. That we protested against this forced union until the Ogoni Native Authority was created in 1947 and placed under the then Rivers Province.
4. That in 1951 we were forcibly included in the Eastern Region of Nigeria where we suffered utter neglect.
5. That we protested against this neglect by voting against the party in power in the Region in 1957, and against the forced union by testimony

before the Willink Commission of Inquiry into Minority Fears in 1958.

6. That this protest led to the inclusion of our nationality in Rivers State in 1967, which State consists of several ethnic nationalities with differing cultures, languages and aspirations.

7. That oil was struck and produced in commercial quantities on our land in 1958 at K. Dere (Bomu oilfield).

8. That oil has been mined on our land since 1958 to this day from the following oilfields: (i) Bomu (ii) Bodo West (iii) Tai (iv) Korokoro (v) Yorla (vi) Lubara Creek and (vii) Afam by Shell Petroleum Development Company (Nigeria) Limited.

9. That in over 30 years of oil mining, the Ogoni nationality have provided the Nigerian nation with a total revenue estimated at over 40 billion Naira (N40 billion) or 30 billion dollars.

10. That in return for the above contribution, the Ogoni people have received NOTHING.

11. That today, the Ogoni people have:

    (i)   No representation whatsoever in ALL institutions of the Federal Government of Nigeria.

    (ii) No pipe-borne water.

    (iii) No electricity.

    (iv) No job opportunities for the citizens in Federal, State, public sector or private sector companies.

    (v)   No social or economic project of the Federal Government.

12. That the Ogoni languages of Gokana and Khana are undeveloped and are about to disappear, whereas other Nigerian languages are being forced on us.

13. That the ethnic policies of successive Federal and State Governments are gradually pushing the Ogoni people to slavery and possible extinction.

14. That the Shell Petroleum Development Company of Nigeria Limited does not employ Ogoni people at a meaningful or any level at all, in defiance of the Federal government's regulations.

15. That the search for oil has caused severe land and food shortages in Ogoni one of the most densely populated areas of Africa (average: 1,500 per square mile; Nigerian national average: 300 per square mile).

16. That neglectful environmental pollution laws and sub-standard inspection techniques of the Federal authorities have led to the complete

degradation of the Ogoni environment, turning our homeland into an ecological disaster.

17. That the Ogoni people lack education, health and other social facilities.
18. That it is intolerable that one of the richest areas of Nigeria should wallow in abject poverty and destitution.
19. That successive Federal administrations have trampled on every minority right enshrined in the Nigerian Constitution to the detriment of the Ogoni and have by administrative structuring and other noxious acts transferred Ogoni wealth exclusively to other parts of the Republic.
20. That the Ogoni people wish to manage their own affairs.

Now, therefore, while reaffirming our wish to remain a part of the Federal Republic of Nigeria, we make demand upon the Republic as follows:

That the Ogoni people be granted POLITICAL AUTONOMY to participate in the affairs of the Republic as a distinct and separate unit by whatever name called, provided that this Autonomy guarantees the following:

(a) Political control of Ogoni affairs by Ogoni people.
(b) The right to the control and use of a fair proportion of Ogoni economic resources for Ogoni development.
(c) Adequate and direct representation as of right in All Nigerian national institutions.
(d) The use and development of Ogoni languages in Ogoni territory.
(e) The full development of Ogoni culture.
(f) The right to religious freedom.
(g) The right to protect the Ogoni environment and ecology from further degradation.

We make the above demand in the knowledge that it does not deny any other ethnic group in the Nigerian Federation of their rights and that it can only conduce to peace, justice and fairplay and hence stability and progress in the Nigerian nation.

We make the above demand in the belief that, as Obafemi Awolowo has written:

In a true Federation, each ethnic group no matter how small, is entitled to the same treatment as any other ethnic group, no matter how large.

We demand these rights as equal members of the Nigerian Federation who contribute and have contributed to the growth of the Federation and have a right to expect full returns from that Federation.

Adopted by general acclaim of the Ogoni people on the 26th day of August, 1990 at Bori, Rivers State.

Signed on behalf of the Ogoni people by:

BABBE: Sgd. HRH Mark Tsaro-Igbara, Gbenemene Babbe; HRH F. M. K. Noryaa, Menebua Ka-Babbe; Chief M. A. M. Tornwe III, JP; Prince J.S. Sangha; Dr Israel Kue; Chief A. M. N. Gua.

GOKANA: Sgd. HRH James P. Bagia, Gberesako XI, Gberemene Gokana; HRH C.A. Mitee, JP., Menebua Numuu; Chief E. N. Kobani, JP, Tonsimene Gokana; Dr B.N. Birabi; Chief Kemte Giadom, JP; Chief S. N. Orage.

NYO-KHANA: Sgd. HRH W. Z. P. Nzidee, Gbenemene Baa I of Nyo-Khana; Dr G. B. Leton, OON,JP; Mr Lekue Lah Loolo; Mr L. E. Mwara; Chief E. A. Apenu; Pastor M. P. Maeba.

KEN-KHANA: Sgd. HRH M. H. S. Eguru, Gbenemene Ken-Khana; HRH C. B. S. Nwikina-Emah III, Menebua Bom; Mr M. C. Daanwii; Chief T. N. Nwieke; Mr Ken Saro-Wiwa; Mr Simeon Idemvor.

TAI: Sgd. HRH B.A. Mballey, Gbenemene Tai; HRH G. N. K. Gininwa, Menebua Tua Tua; Chief J.S. Agbara; Chief D. J. K. Kumbe; Chief Fred Gwezia; HRH A. Demor-Kanni, Menebua Nonwa Tai.

General Babangida and his Council did not only ignore the Bill, but proceeded to split the country into 30 States and 589 local government areas which further marginalized the Ogoni people and brought them closer to extinction.

This act made it clear that appealing to the ethnic majority in Nigeria was an exercise in futility as they were hell-bent on genocide and were merely using the Nigerian nation as a cover for their misdeeds.

They received a further jolt when President Babangida, addressing the United Nations as President of the Organization of African Unity, studiously ignored oil pollution as one of the menaces to the African environment, choosing to mention only desertification, erosion and all such.

The Ogoni were not unmindful of the trends in world history, particularly the break-up of such multi-ethnic States as the Soviet Union and Yugoslavia. They also took into account the fact that the only reason the Nigerian nation can survive today is the oil resource of the Ogoni and other peoples in the delta; that this oil is being mined by European and American investment and technology and being bought by the Americans, Japanese and the Europeans. Therefore, these nations, the most powerful on earth, have a role to play in the drive of the Ogoni for justice and survival.

Therefore, in 1991, Ogoni Chiefs and elders met once again to appeal to the international community:

ADDENDUM TO THE OGONI BILL OF RIGHTS

We, the people of Ogoni, being a separate and distinct ethnic nationality within the Federal Republic of Nigeria, hereby state as follows:

A. That on October 2, 1990 we addressed an "Ogoni Bill of Rights" to the President of the Federal Republic of Nigeria, General Ibrahim Babangida and members of the Armed Forces Ruling Council;

B. That after a one-year wait, the President has been unable to grant us the audience which we sought to have with him in order to discuss the legitimate demands contained in the Ogoni Bill of Rights;

C. That our demands as outlined in the Ogoni Bill of Rights are legitimate, just and our inalienable right and in accord with civilized values worldwide;

D. That the Government of the Federal Republic has continued, since October 2, 1990, to decree measures and implement policies which further marginalize the Ogoni people, denying us political autonomy, our rights to our resources, to the development of our languages and culture, to adequate representation as of right in all Nigerian national institutions and to the protection of our environment and ecology from further degradation;

E. That we cannot sit idly by while we are, as a people, dehumanized and slowly exterminated and driven to extinction even as our rich resources are siphoned off to the exclusive comfort and improvement of other Nigerian communities, and the shareholders of multinational oil companies.

Now, therefore, while re-affirming our wish to remain a part of the Federal Republic of Nigeria, we hereby authorize the Movement for the Survival of Ogoni People (MOSOP) to make representation, for as long as these injustices continue, to the United Nations Commission on Human Rights, the Commonwealth Secretariat, the African Commission on Human and Peoples' Rights, the European Community and all international bodies which have a role to play in the preservation of our nationality, as follows:

1. That the Government of the Federal Republic of Nigeria has, in utter disregard and contempt for human rights, since independence in 1960 till date, denied us our political rights to self-determination, economic rights to our resources, cultural rights to the development of our languages and culture, and social rights to education, health and adequate housing and to representation as of right in national institutions;

2. That, in particular, the Federal Republic of Nigeria has refused to pay us oil royalties and mining rents amounting to an estimated 20 billion US dollars for petroleum mined from our soil for over thirty-three years;

3. That the Constitution of the Federal Republic of Nigeria does not protect any of our rights whatsoever as an ethnic minority of 500,000 in a nation of about 100 million people and that the voting power and military might of the majority ethnic groups have been used remorselessly against us at every point in time;

4. That multinational oil companies, namely Shell (Dutch/ British) and Chevron (American) have severally and jointly devastated our environment and ecology, having flared gas in our villages for 33 years and caused oil spillages, blow-outs etc., and have dehumanized our people, denying them employment and those benefits which industrial organizations in Europe and America routinely contribute to their areas of operation;

5. That the Nigerian elite (bureaucratic, military, industrial and academic) have turned a blind eye and a deaf ear to these acts of dehumanization by the ethnic majority and have colluded with all the agents of destruction aimed at us;

6. That we cannot seek restitution in the courts of law in Nigeria as the act of expropriation of our rights and resources has been institutionalized in the 1979 and 1989 Constitutions of the Federal Republic of Nigeria, which Constitutions were acts of a Constituent Assembly imposed by a military regime and do not, in any way, protect minority rights or bear resemblance

to the tacit agreement made at Nigerian independence;

7. That the Ogoni people abjure violence in their just struggle for their rights within the Federal Republic of Nigeria but will, through every lawful means, and for as long as is necessary, fight for social justice and equity for themselves and their progeny, and in particular demand political autonomy as a distinct and separate unit within the Nigerian nation with full right to (i) control Ogoni political affairs, (ii) use at least fifty per cent of Ogoni economic resources for Ogoni development; (iii) protect the Ogoni environment and ecology from from further degradation; (iv) ensure the full restitution of the harm done to the health of our people by the flaring of gas, oil spillages, oil blow-outs, etc. by the following oil companies: Shell, Chevron and their Nigerian accomplices.

8. That without the intervention of the international community, the Government of the Federal Republic of Nigeria and the ethnic majority will continue these noxious policies until the Ogoni people are obliterated from the face of the earth. Adopted by general acclaim of the Ogoni people on the 26th day of August 1991 at Bori, Rivers State of Nigeria. Signed on behalf of the Ogoni people by:

BABBE: Sgd. HRH Mark Tsaro-Igbara, Gbenemene Babbe; HRH F. M. K. Noryaa, Menebua Ka-Babbe; Chief M. A. M. Tornwe III, JP; Prince J.S. Sangha; Dr Israel Kue; Chief A. M. N. Gua.

GOKANA: Sgd. HRH James P. Bagia, Gberesako XI, Gberemene Gokana; Chief E. N. Kobani, JP, Tonsimene Gokana; Dr B.N. Birabi; Chief Kemte Giadom, JP; Chief S. N. Orage.

NYO-KHANA: Sgd. HRH W. Z. P. Nzidee, Gbenemene Baa I of Nyo-Khana; Dr G. B. Leton, OON, JP; Mr Lekue Lah Loolo; Mr L. E. Mwara; Chief E. A. Apenu; Pastor M. P. Maeba.

KEN-KHANA: Sgd. HRH M. H. S. Eguru, Gbenemene Ken-Khana; HRH C. B. S. Nwikina-Emah III, Menebua Bom; Mr M. C. Daanwii; Chief T. N. Nwieke; Mr Ken Saro-Wiwa; Mr Simeon Idemyor.

TAI: Sgd. HRH B.A. Mballey, Gbenemene Tai; HRH G. N. K. Gininwa,

Menebua Tua Tua; Chief J.S. Agbara; Chief D. J. K. Kumbe; Chief Fred Gwezia; HRH A. Demor-Kanni, Menebua Nonwa Tai.

I wish, as a writer, to add my voice to this appeal of the Ogoni people to the international community. This study has shown, convincingly I hope, the collusion of multi-national oil companies and the ethnic majority in Nigeria in the total destruction of the Ogoni nation.

The travails of the Ogoni people are probably repeated many times over in different parts of the world. Taken together, such violence, for that is what it is, practised on weak and defenceless peoples, demeans the human race. It is a joint responsibility to put an end to it.

Over the past thirty years, I have made representation, in writing and in person, to the power elite in Nigeria to put an end to the misery, or at least to mitigate the harm which they do to the Ogoni. I have not only failed to convince them; each appeal has been followed by further acts of genocide.

These genocidal actions have been condoned by all Nigerians. Even well-known Nigerian writers, who would ordinarily be expected to decry these actions have lent support, by their silence, to them. In one case, following the publication of my book, *On A Darkling Plain: An Account of the Nigerian Civil War,* where I raised the matter of the denial of the rights of the Ogoni to their resources, Kole Omotoso, a writer well-known for his liberal views, asked, in a review of the book:

> *how true is it to say that the riverine areas 'produce' oil? Are*
> *we to assume that the people of the riverine areas produce oil*
> *in the same way that the Ondo people produce cocoa or Kano*
> *produce cotton?*
> *If this were the way of thinking of what comes out of the soil*
> *of the riverine areas, the distribution of the resultant revenue*
> *would have been different.*

Dr Omotoso did not ask if the Ondo farmers had been deprived of their land. Nor did he ask if the planting of cocoa had poisoned the air of the Yoruba people in the Ondo area. Or whether Yoruba farmers had been denied the ownership of the fruit of their farms.

Thus, even the purest minds in Nigeria are marked by their greed for oil money and their insensitivity to the suffering of the minorities.

This insensitivity owes itself to the ethnic nature of Nigerian society.

Ethnocentrism blinds even the best men to injustice, discrimination, even genocide perpetrated against those who are not of their own ethnic groups.

The ethnic majority in Nigeria count it as nothing to order the murder of peasants protesting the high-handedness of a multi-national oil company as happened in the Etche ethnic group of Rivers State when a detachment of Nigerian Mobile Police Force mowed down 14 men and women, and burnt down the village of Umuechem. No one has been punished for this dastardly crime. The Nigerian Police Force or the Nigerian Army can mow down ethnic minority protesters easily because in most cases members of the Forces sent on such duty would be perfect strangers in the area and would consider themselves as protecting their own ethnic interest in killing as many people as possible. In some cases, soldiers and policemen might find their religion no barrier whatsoever to harming people among whom oil is found.

The ethnic majority in Nigeria are anxious to benefit as much as possible from oil, knowing full well that oil is a wasting asset. This is why Nigeria's huge earnings from oil are being frittered away or committed to expensive projects in the non-oil producing areas of the country. The idea is that when oil runs out, as it will surely do, such areas will have all the benefits of the oil industry, leaving the oil-producing areas with a blighted environment.

It is left for the reader to decide whether a group of people who have no conscience, are opportunistic, who vary rules to suit their immediate design, whether such people will, in the absence of oil, be willing to cater in any measure for the oil-bearing areas and those who reside there. There is no doubt in my mind at all that they will not care a hoot for such people especially as they find that they are powerless.

Today, the ethnic majorities in Nigeria enjoy a multiplicity of bureaucracies which they do not need, agricultural outfits, a myriad Universities, abundant schools, television and radio stations, etc. But they will fight to the death anyone who suggests that any of these be extended to the minorities who own the oil which have made these blessings possible.

The ethnic majority in Nigeria are behaving true to type: persisting in evil (as they did during the slave trade) and waiting for other nations to COMPEL them to mend their ways.

In the circumstance, only the international community and well-meaning individuals acting in their personal capacity, or collectively where possible, can stop this wholesale and mindless destruction of the environment, this genocide.

The profile of the Ogoni today is of a proud, independent,distinct ethnic group numbering an estimated 500,000, christian, richly blessed by nature, inhabiting the south-east of Nigeria. Their land gushes with petroleum and natural gas, an estimated US100 billion dollars of which has been extracted over the last 33 years by two racist, brutal and callous multi-national oil companies - Shell (Dutch/British) and Chevron (American) whose activities have completely devastated the local environment and ecology. All wildlife is dead, plant life is endangered, the rivers and streams and air are polluted by the oil spillages, blow-outs and gas flares of 33 years; the land has been rendered infertile by acid rain. All primary schools are closed, educated youths find no jobs, children die of malnutrition and kwashiokor; there is no pipe-borne water, electricity, hospital or industry.

Over them sits, vampire-like, a bogus, debt-ridden Nigeria with a fraudulent, undemocratic Constitution operated by an ethnic majority which has expropriated and wasted Ogoni resources for over 30 years. This ethnic majority, bound by none of the rules of modern, civilized, international society has bullied and tortured them since independence and now waits to deal them the final death-blow.

The situation is tragic. The question is, will the international community fold its arms and allow this twenty-first century genocide?

I urge upon the international community a ten-point course of action:

1. Prevail on the American Government to stop buying Nigerian oil. It is stolen property.

2. Prevail on Shell and Chevron to stop flaring gas in Ogoni and other oil-producing areas.

3. Prevail on the Federal Government of Nigeria to honour the rights of the Ogoni people to self-determination and AUTONOMY.

4. Prevail on the Federal Government of Nigeria to pay to the Ogoni people all royalties and mining rents collected on oil mined from Ogoni since 1958, according to the revenue allocation formula agreed before independence.

5. Prevail on the World Bank and the International Monetary Fund to stop giving all loans whose repayment depends on the exploitation of Ogoni oil resources to the Federal Government of Nigeria.

6. Send urgent medical and other aid to the Ogoni people.

7. Prevail on the United Nations, the Organization of African Unity and the Commonwealth of Nations to either get the Federal Government of Nigeria to implement the human rights declarations of these organizations, face sanctions or be expelled from them.

8. Prevail on European and American Governments to stop giving aid and credit to the Federal Government of Nigeria as aid and credit only go to encourage the further dehumanization of the Ogoni people and other minorities.

9. Prevail on European and American Governments to grant political refugee status to all Ogoni people seeking protection from political persecution and genocide at the hands of the Federal Government of Nigeria.

10. Prevail on Shell and Chevron to pay compensation to the Ogoni people for ruining the Ogoni environment and the health of Ogoni men, women and children.

The matter is urgent. I live in the hope that somewhere in this world, good still exists and that it will prevail over evil.

If nothing is done now, the Ogoni people will be extinct within ten years.

People of the world, I appeal to you in the name of God to help stop this genocide of the Ogoni people NOW!

THE END